A lad a BBQ and a Pillar of Salt

WRITTEN BY
MALC' HALLIDAY

CARTOONS BY
IAN POTTER

Scripture Union

Scripture Union, 207–209 Queensway, Bletchley, MK2 2EB, England
www.scriptureunion.org.uk
info@scriptureunion.org.uk

First published 2001
ISBN 1 85999367 2

British Library Cataloguing-in-Publication Data. A catalogue
record for this book is available from the British Library.

Printed and bound in Great Britain by Creative Print and Design
(Wales), Ebbw Vale.

WHAT'S WHERE?

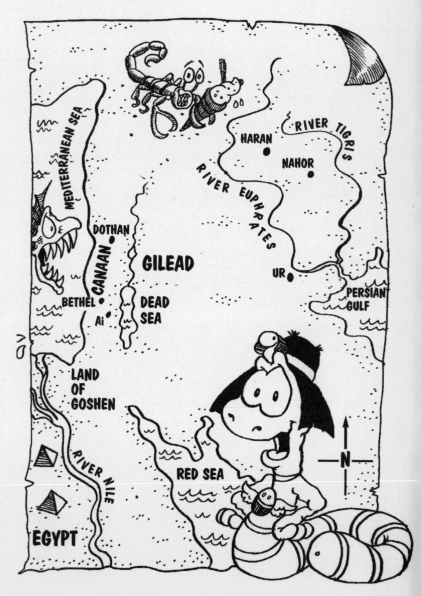

YOUR GUIDES

SHIMEI THE SMELLI

Alright! I'm Shimei. How are ya? I'd just like to say, 'Nice one for buying this book!' I'll be guiding you through the ins and outs, the ups and downs, the highs and lows, the tops and bottoms... not that there are many bottoms in here. You get the idea. Anyway, I'll be showing you around the book, and to help me with this enormous task is Benji.

BENJI THE BOOKWORM

Hi! I'm Benji – I've managed to worm my way (geddit?) into this book because Shimei is hopeless with numbers. He also smells awful, but that's another story. When you see me holding up a sign, if you like you can get your Bible out and read the 'official' version of the story.

INTRODUCTION

Before the big floods came, Noah had rescued all the animals and his family and set off on a world cruise. But what follows is not his story.

When the waters had subsided and the land had dried up, Noah's sons (Japheth, Ham and Shem) set about growing crops, tending the herds and repopulating the world in an age-old manner that has never gone out of fashion. But this is not their story.

After Noah's sons came a variety of people with strange names. Tubal and Tiras, Havilah and Sabtecah, Uz and Phoenix Chi Brooklyn[1], the list goes on and on. But what you are about to read is not their story.

However, Shem did have a son called Arphaxad. Arphaxad's son had sons who had sons who had sons until one day a man called Terah said, 'We'll call this one Abram.' This is HIS story. (You could say it was the history of his story but we won't bother.)

Abram, the great-great-great-great-great-great-great-great grandson of Noah (trust me) had done all right for himself. The family were nicely settled in Ur and had made their money by trading with those who passed through on their way from

---

[1] OK, I made that one up.

Mesopotamia to the Mediterranean (and back again if they were lucky).

They were a happy family, and when Terah decided to move to a desirable plot of land in Canaan the family went with him. However, just as in a supermarket when you're heading for the one thing you need, something else catches your eye and you buy that instead, so it was that when the family came to Haran – 550 miles from where they set out – they decided enough was enough and stopped there instead.

Abram and his wife Sarai expected to end their days in Haran. They had enough flocks and herds to keep them comfortable in their old age and life was good. True, they'd never had the children they wanted, but Abram was seventy-five now, and Sarai sixty-five, so clearly that was out of the question.

D'OH! WHO NEEDS KIDS WITH ALL THIS LOT?

However, as it turned out, when Terah had set off for Canaan, it had not simply been the whimsical idea of an old man – God had been doing the nudging. And as history shows, when God has a good idea, he doesn't let it go until he's seen it through. So, Abram, as you look out on your family and possessions, don't order the pipe, slippers and rocking chair just yet. Things are about to change...

1 THE PROMISE

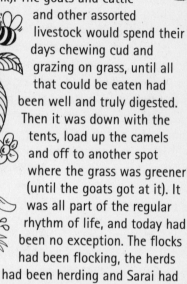

GENESIS 12:1-9

It had been the usual kind of day for your run-of-the-mill Nomads (wandering folk). The goats and cattle and other assorted livestock would spend their days chewing cud and grazing on grass, until all that could be eaten had been well and truly digested. Then it was down with the tents, load up the camels and off to another spot where the grass was greener (until the goats got at it). It was all part of the regular rhythm of life, and today had been no exception. The flocks had been flocking, the herds had been herding and Sarai had been doing whatever it was that she got up to in that tent all day. Abram didn't like to ask – although it always seemed to result in food appearing at mealtimes, so he was very grateful. Yes, just a typical day and then came... The Voice.

Abram looked round, but no one was there. Maybe his nephew Lot was playing tricks? But it hadn't sounded like Lot. This was a voice of power, majesty, authority and... suddenly the penny dropped, and Abram began to listen very carefully. When the Maker of heaven and earth decides to hold a conversation with you, it's a good idea to listen. Well, not so much a conversation, as God told Abram what to do. That's kind of a thing with God–

he does expect to be obeyed. But Abram was still the one who had to decide to do the obeying.

Abram was being told to go. To round up the family and flocks and move on. Haran was a *good* land but it wasn't *God's* land for Abram. God had something better in mind, and made Abram a promise. Not just any kind of promise, but an earth-shattering, mind-numbing, make-you-cross-eyed sort of promise.

'You,' said God, to a rather astonished, not to say gob-smacked, Abram, 'will be the head of a nation. You will have a family that will fill a country and your name will be up there with the greats. I am going to do things through your family that will mean the whole world will give thanks that there was a man called Abram.'

If the thought of children seemed a bit unlikely to Abram – him being seventy-five years old and Sarai being sixty-five – he was too polite to say so.

The next thing Sarai, Lot and the rest of the family knew, Abram was rushing through the camp giving orders. 'Come on! Drink up your sandwiches and eat your lemonade! Load up the tents! Pack away the camels! And don't get the hump – it wasn't my idea!' Most of what he said in this excited state was fairly unintelligible, but the message got through: they were on the move.

9

So it was that Abram and his family completed the journey that Terah had intended to make all those years ago. Terah, you will recall (you are keeping up, aren't you?), had meant to take his family to Canaan, but after a tiring first leg of the journey had found the town of Haran and decided to stop for a little rest. The little rest turned into a short holiday and the short holiday became 'We'll stop here for the time being' which eventually became 'Canaan... what do we want to go there for?'

As soon as Abram and the gang had crossed the 'Canaan Welcomes Careful Camels' sign, one thing became obvious. They were not alone. Strangely enough, the whole of Canaan was full of Canaanites, who weren't likely to take kindly to a whole tribe of people walking in and saying 'This is our land now.' It was all very well Abram saying that God had told them to go and live in Canaan, but had he told the Canaanites? Still, God was in control, and somehow Abram knew that it would all turn out alright. He'd no idea how, but he knew it would.

CANAAN
TWINNED WITH
MILTON KEYNES

For the time being, the Canaanites seemed quite happy to let these foreigners wander around. There was grass to spare, and they could afford to be hospitable (after all, they didn't know that Abram and the rest were planning to stick around for a while). As Abram waited for the next set of instructions, he spent a lot of time talking to God, reminding himself just who was in charge of this expedition. Every time he stopped he made an altar – a place of worship and sacrifice. Now, these altars wouldn't get you through GCSE technology and design. They were just made of bits of stone and mud. But to anybody who passed by, they were a powerful sign – a sign that there had been people in this land who served the living God. Of course, the more the altars grew, the more likely the Canaanites were to pick up on the idea that these visitors weren't just passing through.

One of those altars had been built at a place called 'Ai' (pronounced 'Aaaaaaaaaaaaaaaaaaayeeeeee'.

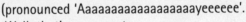

Well, that's one way to pronounce it) and some time later, Abram found himself back there. He had kept going because: a) God hadn't told him what the next stage of the plan was yet; b) the sheep, goats and cattle needed fresh grass at an alarming rate; and c) he hadn't got any better ideas at that particular moment. So far,

GENESIS 13:1-13

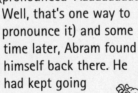

11

things had gone relatively smoothly – especially with the relatives. Sarai still couldn't quite believe that Abram had got it right about having a family (not if it involved her, at any rate) but she didn't argue and just went where he went. Lot, too, had a lot of respect for his Uncle Abe, and even if he would have preferred the life of a settled settler to that of a wandering, ermmm, wanderer, he was prepared to give it a go. But this is real life and all this peace, harmony and goodwill was too good to last. Which was why it didn't.

The grass was the problem. Not the colour, the texture or the flavour of it. Just the quantity – there wasn't enough.

Abram had his flocks, Lot had his and there was the little matter of those who already lived in the land – the Canaanites and Perizzites – who had been managing quite nicely before these strangers came along. It was the shepherds who started grumbling first. Abram's were falling out with Lot's over where the grass was greener and who had the right to it when they found it. If Abram knew anything about anything, it was that if you don't stop the hired hands from complaining, before you know it there's dissension, revolt, riot – all in all a mess. Something had to be done.

Abram and Lot reviewed the situation. Maybe by staying together they were making things worse. It was hard to do, but for the sake of family harmony Abram suggested they go their separate ways. There was

plenty of land available and he gave Lot first pick. Lot looked around and saw how green the Jordan valley was – it would make an ideal spot for building up his crops and establishing his own family business. The city of Sodom was nearby – extremely handy if you ran out of anything, like toothpaste or bubblebath, or were at a loose end on a Friday night. Yes, thought Lot, that's the place for me. So he took his cows and goats and sheep, told his servants to stop causing trouble, and off he went.

Abram watched him go with a heavy heart. Lot was like the son he had never had. Although he was only going to be just down the valley, who knew when he would see him again?

Abram was thinking these thoughts when it suddenly occurred to him that this was surely a step backwards. God had promised him a family and yet here was one of the only relatives he had, disappearing over the horizon with his sheep trotting down the valley behind him wagging their tails. Surely there was something wrong with the 'master plan'? It would have been easy for Abram to start having doubts, wondering whether he'd brought his wife on nothing more than an extended camping holiday. That's when God spoke again, and with Lot several miles down the valley, Abram had no suspicions at all about who was speaking this time.

'Abram,' said God, 'take a good look at all this land. It will all be yours, and your family will be so numerous nobody will be able to count them. Keep on walking through this land – it will be your land. Trust me.'

Trust him! Abram had no children, he'd left his own country, his nephew had wandered off with half his herds and the Canaanites and Perizzites were continually telling him 'We were here first, matey! So watch it!' Of course he was going to trust God – if God didn't pull it off then Abram was well and truly sunk. With these thoughts, Abram packed up his tent again and set off for Hebron.

2 A RIGHT ROYAL SCRAP

GENESIS 13:14 – 14:24

Meanwhile there was trouble brewing – and it wasn't a storm in a teacup either. In the lands around Canaan there were lots of kings and not a lot of land. This was a recipe for disaster. Being a king – for those of you who have never tried – is a bit like eating in the school canteen. You've collected your tray and filled it up quite happily with a dinoburger, some beans and plenty of chips. You are walking along ready to pay Mrs Grotbucket, the fearsome dinnerlady on the till, when you see that Tommy Simpkins has got a bigger dinoburger, crispier chips and more beans than you. This doesn't seem fair. You could just say 'Oh well, tomorrow is another day... maybe I'll get more then.' But no, you decide to pinch Tommy's dinner and eat that as well. Because you are bigger, meaner and rougher than sweet young Tommy, this is not a problem (well, it is for Tommy, but that's another matter).

That's how the kings around Canaan acted. They got what they wanted, and they wanted what somebody else had as well. In fact, they were greedy. If they'd been in your dinner queue, they wouldn't have stopped at Tommy Simpkins. Oh no. Mrs Grotbucket or not, they would have made their way down the whole canteen taking whatever they liked. You might think that seventeen burgers and a wheely-bin full of chips was enough for anyone, but they just went on taking more and more.

So it was that in Abram's day, if one lot of kings wasn't attacking another, then there was something seriously wrong. It was hard to keep up: the Elamites attacked the Sodomites; Kings Bera and Birsha were seen off by King Tidal (you might say they were 'swept away by the waves of invading armies') and King Chedorlaomer (pronounced 'Sir') conquered the Repha-ites, the Zuz-ites, the Em-ites and the Hor-ites. Had the Israel-ites been around at this time, they'd have been pretty scared (but they won't exist until a lot further on in this book).

Meanwhile King Tidal and his allies had found themselves washed up on the shores of Sodom and Gomorrah and soon the cities, their food, their wealth and their people were free no longer. Lot, who you will remember had recently settled nearby, got caught up in the backwash and was taken prisoner. Indeed, Lot's 'lot' was not a happy one.

When Abram heard the news, he knew he had to do something. Lot was family after all and, well you can't let any Tom, Dick and Tidal mess around with your family can you?

16

Abram took his servants (those who were handy in a battle at any rate), surrounded King Tidal and his gang and mopped up the lot overnight. Lot was rescued, the people of Sodom went free and Abram had all the loot which had been taken by the kings.

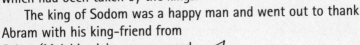

The king of Sodom was a happy man and went out to thank Abram with his king-friend from Salem (Melchizedek – pronounced slowly). It was a serious moment,

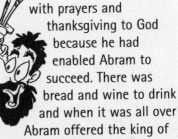

with prayers and thanksgiving to God because he had enabled Abram to succeed. There was bread and wine to drink and when it was all over Abram offered the king of Salem ten per cent of all the wealth he had gained from his battle, and returned everything belonging to the king of Sodom. You would think that Abram was entitled to a bit of the booty,

but he'd meant it when he said that he would trust God. Any wealth, riches or other goodies Abram possessed had to be his because God had provided them and for no other reason.

It was some time later that God showed Abram that he had been right to refuse the gold of Sodom. God spoke to him one night and promised him future wealth and protection. But there was only one thing that Abram really wanted – children. Children to care for him in his old(er) age, children to bring their innocent laughter and songs into his family and most especially children

GENESIS 15:1–21

to inherit his wealth. Abram had a lot of wealth to be inherited. The tradition of his people, if there were no children to leave all your worldly goods to, was to give all your money, goats, possessions and wives to your most trusted servant. Eliezer, who looked after the running of Abram's household, was a good man. He was loyal and conscientious, and if a servant had to inherit then he would be a good choice. But it was not what Abram wanted. He was quite prepared to leave Eliezer his second-best tent or suggest that he take his pick of the camels, but for him to have everything didn't seem right somehow. Abram was not a happy Nomad.

God knew it was not going to work out this way. 'You *will* have a son,' he told Abram. But there was more. God told Abram to look up. 'Count the stars,' God said. Abram had got as far as 2,372 when he stopped and said, 'This is silly. I can't count them, there's far too many.'

18

'Exactly,' said God, with the sort of delight a teacher shows when Johnny finally grasps how to do long multiplication. 'And you will have so many children, grandchildren (and so on) that you won't be able to count those either.' Abram looked up again. He couldn't see *how* it would happen and he didn't know *when* it would happen, but something deep inside told him that it *would* happen – because *God* had said so.

Some time later, God reminded Abram again that he had brought him all the way from Ur so that he could live in the land of Canaan and it would be his. Abram was far too polite to point out that he would hardly have forgotten a thing

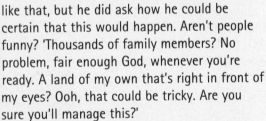

like that, but he did ask how he could be certain that this would happen. Aren't people funny? 'Thousands of family members? No problem, fair enough God, whenever you're ready. A land of my own that's right in front of my eyes? Ooh, that could be tricky. Are you sure you'll manage this?'

God didn't show Abram the future, give him the land of Canaan or a clip round the ear for being so cheeky. Instead he reminded him just how powerful and majestic he was. He told Abram to bring animals to sacrifice. Abram brought a cow, a goat, a ram, a dove and a baby pigeon. He cut them in half (messy with a goat, very tricky with a baby pigeon so God told him not to bother) and laid them on the ground in two rows making a sort of passageway between the bits. (Remember DON'T try this at home – a dog is for life not just for acting out of biblical sacrifices.)

The sun set and Abram sat... and waited. The sky grew darker, the wind started to blow. Abram was alone in the fields with a pile of dead animals. It didn't feel safe. In fact it was a little bit frightening, so Abram did the obvious thing – he fell asleep! While he slept, God spoke again. He foretold of the family who would be taken prisoner and forced into slavery, and that there would come a time when they would be free to come and live in this land. It was a long way off in the future, but Abram needed to be reassured that God would do what he had promised – however long it seemed to take.

Abram woke just in time to see a smouldering pot and a fire making their way between the rows of dead animals. He watched with perhaps not quite as much amazement as you would have done. We'd probably think 'Strange and spooky!' Abram thought 'A sign that God is really going to do all that he says.'

Meanwhile, back at the tents, what about Sarai? It was all very well Abram saying that he was going to have a son, but if truth be told, *he* wasn't going to doing much of the 'having' at all. Sarai would be the one who had to go through the whole uncomfortable, painful, messy, wonderful process of giving birth. Of course she had to be pregnant first... and, well, it just wasn't happening. Time ticked on, and it was getting harder and harder to believe that she was going to have a baby. But Sarai knew how important it was to Abram to have a son, and so she made an astounding suggestion: 'Abram, sleep with my slave.'

Hagar the slave was younger and more likely to have children. It seemed such a good idea. After all, she was only a slave. Slaves had no rights, and if Hagar had a baby, Sarai could take it for her own. No questions asked. No members of the Canaanite police knocking on your tent-flap late at night wanting to ask you questions. It was all perfectly legal. The fact that it rescued Sarai from all the pain of giving birth[2] obviously never crossed her mind... honest.

GENESIS 16:1–5

---

[2] If you would like to know exactly what it is like to give birth, try the following: Take your top lip and pull it until it completely covers the top half of your head and you'll be somewhere close!

Having a good idea is one thing, but living with the consequences is another. Once Hagar was pregnant and the baby was growing inside her by the day, it was hard for Sarai to ignore. Every time she saw Hagar, she was reminded of what she'd been unable to do for Abram. At the same time, Hagar was exploiting her situation like mad. She never lost a chance to remind Sarai of the facts.

Who knows, in the back of her mind, perhaps she thought Abram would get rid of Sarai and make her his real wife. It was very difficult. Hagar was becoming more and more hostile to Sarai, Sarai had just about had enough and Abram was stuck in the middle: he wanted the baby, but he wanted his wife Sarai to be happy as well. What had he done? And what could he do now?

If this was a TV soap, there would be a close-up of Abram's agonised expression and that drummer would start up at this point.

Anyway something had to be done (cue drummer).

> Incidentally – how does that drummer always know where to be at the end of EastEnders, and how come you never see him? Life – what a mysterious thing it is.

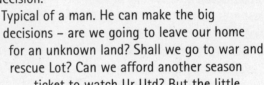

Abram snapped. Obviously not literally – he'd have to have been a Rice Krispie Cake (which he wasn't). But in the end he told Sarai, 'Hagar's your slave, so whatever you want to do with her, it's your decision.'

Typical of a man. He can make the big decisions – are we going to leave our home for an unknown land? Shall we go to war and rescue Lot? Can we afford another season ticket to watch Ur Utd? But the little decisions all become the woman's responsibility – what shall we eat tonight? Who's going to get the washing done? Can we afford a bigger tent? What shall we do about the servant problem?

Sarai didn't need telling twice. No job Hagar did was good enough for her, and no requests for a rest 'because of the baby' were allowed. If all work and no play makes Jack a dull boy, then Hagar was set to become a very dull boy called Jack indeed. In the end, she couldn't take any more and ran until she could run no more. She didn't know where she was going, or what she was going to do.

Fortunately God did. 'Go back,' he said. Not really what Hagar wanted to hear. She probably didn't want to know that the baby she was

23

carrying was going to be like a wild donkey (although the way he kicked inside her, she probably already had a good idea) but God told her that as well. He persuaded her that returning was the right thing to do and so Hagar went back. She gave birth to a baby boy back at the camp and called him Ishmael. (Which is an anagram of male-ish but I'm sure there was no doubt that the baby really was a boy. The real meaning of the name was 'God hears'.)

It looked as if God's promise was about to be met. Abram was eighty-six years old and at last he had the son he had been promised. Or had he... ?

³ A WHOLE LOT OF TROUBLE

GENESIS 17:1-26

Thirteen years passed by. Abram was not getting any younger (which would have been really surprising) and Ishmael was now a teenager – although 'the teenager' hadn't been invented and wouldn't be for several thousand years. So, if Ishmael was moody, sulky and didn't talk much to his parents, but spent hours in his tent listening to 'loud' music, then nobody was going to be able to explain why. In fact in Abram's time, you went straight from carefree child to responsible adult in one jump. Something which most of us don't manage to do in a lifetime.

Abram must have dreamt, while he watched his son grow, of all that God had promised coming true through Ishmael and his children and his children's

children and his children's children's... well you get the idea. But something Abram was being a bit slow in realising was that you can't make *God's* plan happen *your* way. If God is going to do something, he will do it *his* way, in *his* time and nothing else will do. God made this clear one day when he had another little word with Abram.

God came to remind Abram of the promise he had made and to reassure him that he would keep it. As a sign, he wanted Abram to change his name. Just a little change but one that made all the difference. God wanted an extra syllable – ha – in his name. 'AbraHAm' sounds a bit like the Hebrew for 'Father of many nations'. Presumably 'Abram' sounds a bit like the Hebrew for 'Fthr mn ntns' which didn't mean much to anybody, and wasn't particularly easy to say. The new name would be the sign that God was going to do what he had said he would do. So she wasn't left out, Sarai became 'Sarah'. Notice here the 'ha' goes backwards. Put them together and what have you got?

Which is probably what Abraham and Sarah were thinking, even if they didn't say it out loud. Especially when God told them that Sarah would have the baby he had promised. The whole Hagar-Ishmael saga was not what God had intended at all. Abraham was nearly a hundred, and the thought of nappies drying between the tents, baby-gunge all over his best robes and having to set up an 'OAPs and toddlers' group was more than he could really take in.

'Ha ha ha,' Abraham went. 'Ha ha ha ha ha.' He wasn't trying out the new syllable in his name – he was laughing. He reckoned that it was better to laugh than to cry, which was the other thing he felt like doing.

'No!' said God. 'I mean it. But I won't forget Ishmael. You did it wrong, but I'll see him right.

Nevertheless, this time next year there'll be another baby, another boy, and he will be called Isaac.'

In the middle of all this, Abraham had been commanded by God to do something else to prove that his family, friends and slaves were committed to God's ways. It was just a little thing, a mark, a sign that would remind them of God's special friendship with them.

It was called 'Circumcision' (pronounced 'Ouch'). Now, how can I explain this? Well, you know that boys are different from girls (and I'm not talking dirty fingernails and an allergy to soap here)? Well, it's where they are most different that the circum-thingy took place. Abraham had to take a knife and cut off the bit of skin at the end of the difference. There are all kinds of good medical reasons for doing this, but for Abraham, his tribe and all his descendants, it became their mark of belonging – belonging to God. With baby boys it was done when they were eight days old. No problems there. At that age you don't

DAD, THIS CIRCUMCISION IDEA, CAN'T WE JUST GIVE IT 'THE CHOP'?

AFRAID NOT SON! I'M PRETTY 'CUT UP' ABOUT IT MYSELF!

remember much, and even if it hurt, you'd soon forget. But Abraham was ninety-nine, and he and all the men had to be done too. No anaesthetics, medi-wipes or pain-numbing drugs... only a large knife. Just imagine... or better still don't.

A few months later, Abraham had visitors. Three men from the East bearing gifts... no sorry, scrub that, wrong story. Three men, anyway. Abraham saw them standing nearby and something told him that this wasn't just any Tom, Dick and Gabriel passing through, but

GENESIS 18:1-15

could be somebody quite important. He rushed to meet them, and invited them in. He brought them water to wash their feet. Travelling in those days meant getting dust everywhere, especially in-between the toes, where it was a right pain to get out. He offered them food. Mind you it was all very well him saying, 'Stay for lunch, we'd love to have you,' but it was Sarah he went running to saying, 'Get your pinny on! We've got visitors.'

BEEF *AND* MILK...! I'LL NEED TO MILK IT BEFORE I COOK IT!

Honestly, some men (well – most men actually). They had beef, yoghurt and milk. In fact, if they'd included fries on the menu they could have been eating at *Sarah's Cowburgers*, with a house special and thick strawberry shake. Times change – but not that much, clearly.

Abraham didn't know it, but one of the three men was actually God carrying a message (there's something about God and 'threes' but that's another thought for another time). It was a message for Sarah. She was still in the tent, washing up, making the coffee, and looking for that box of after-dinner mints left over from the last time they'd had guests. Suddenly she heard her name mentioned. The visitor (who *we* know was God) promised that next time he passed that way, Sarah would have a baby.

From the tent came a snort, then a chuckle, some stifled sniggers and then what could only be described as a guffaw – a gale of laughter loud enough to twitch the guy ropes and rattle the tent pegs.

'Why is she laughing?' asked God. 'Does she think it's beyond me?'

'She probably thinks it's beyond me,' thought Abraham, but he said nothing. Sarah appeared at the door of the tent, trying to look solemn and pretend that the tears she was wiping away from her face were to do with the mountains of washing-up and weren't evidence of suppressed hysterics.

'Laugh?' asked Sarah. 'Not me.'

Bad move. Don't try to be clever with God, and don't tell him pork pies[3]. Two life-rules which many forget at their peril. There was no quibbling with God – he knew Sarah had laughed, but he also knew that, come next year, she'd be laughing for a completely different reason.

---

[3] Lies.

29

GENESIS 18:16 – 19:30

The visitors got up to leave and Abraham walked for a while with them as they made their way along the valley towards Sodom. If you cast your mind back, dear reader, to an earlier part of our story, you will remember that this is where Lot went to settle after he had left his Uncle Abram (as he was then). The land was fertile, there was plenty of grazing for the herds, and life should have been good. Unfortunately the town of Sodom, and its neighbour Gomorrah, were not nice places to be. They were places of sin, vice, corruption and despicable goings on. Towns where, if you invited the neighbours in for supper, you checked their pockets for cutlery before they left (if you were still alive to check them that is). Places that made the tackiest soap-opera look like 'Songs of Praise'. The only thing worshipped was self-interest, and if you went out alone at night you wouldn't be alone – or alive – for long. All in all, *not* a nice neighbourhood.

30

Well, God had had enough, and as he walked with Abraham, he talked of his plans for the cities. If it was as bad as God believed, then that would be the end of Sodom, Gomorrah and everyone in them. As God continued to talk, his two companions set out for the city of Sodom to check it out. Abraham, thinking about Lot and his family, asked God whether, if there were fifty good people in Sodom, they would have to suffer along with everybody else? God's considered opinion was that no, the city *could* be saved to protect fifty good people.

Abraham took a deep breath and decided to haggle. Now, bargaining with God might seem like a dumb move but since Abraham had already tried to outwit him in the matter of the promised son and heir, and Sarah had lied to God, Abraham didn't really think he had that much to lose. The conversation went something like this...

'If there are forty-five good people, will the city be spared?'

'OK.'

'Forty?'

'Alright.'

'Thirty?'

'Er, fair enough.'

'Twenty?'

'It's a deal.'

'Ten?'

'Done.'

That was probably as far as he could push it, thought Abraham the expert haggler. Surely that should cover Lot and his family. It might have crossed Abraham's mind that he seemed to spend a

lot of time getting his nephew out of
trouble, which was surely beyond the
boundaries of an uncle's
responsibilities (restricted to occasional
trips to the zoo and £10 at Harvest-
time, Christmas not having been
invented yet).

Meanwhile, the two men with God
(who were really angels – had you
guessed?) had arrived at Sodom,
and who should they see but Lot
who had inherited his uncle's gift of
hospitality. The angels tried to say
that they would stay elsewhere but Lot
insisted, and so for the second time that
day they were sitting down to a twelfth-
century-BC cowburger.

The people of Sodom noticed the
arrival of strangers in town – it
was such a rarity. Most
people had the sense to take
the long way round rather
than risk a trip through
Sodom's streets. Visitors
meant new opportunities for
nastiness, unpleasant goings on
and indescribable wickedness
(so I won't try). Sure enough
as Lot's guests finished their
meal there was a banging on the
door and shouts of, 'Bring them out here, Lot. We've got
plans for them.' Lot's training in social etiquette stretched
as far as knowing that 'offering guests[4] to the neighbours for

---

[4] The same should apply to daughters too.

mass ravaging and
abuse' was just not on.
He went outside and
started talking to
the mob
surrounding his
house, but obviously
hadn't read the
footnote at the bottom
of the previous page,

and suggested that the people of Sodom could have just as much
fun with his two girls. What his daughters thought about this, we
will never know, but fortunately for them, the crowd refused.

They had set their minds on an
evening of debauchery
with the strangers and
nothing less would do. The
crowd was getting restless, and
Lot couldn't hold them off for
ever. Suddenly there was a huge
rush towards the door. Getting past
Lot and into the house was going
to be a doddle. Well – a doddle if
your two guests didn't happen to be a
pair of angelic beings. Quick as a

flash, they pulled Lot inside, and
turned off the
streetlights for
everyone else. The
whole mob was
blind, so blind they
couldn't even find the
door, let alone open
it and find the
strangers.

Inside the house, Lot listened to the cries of, 'Who turned out the lights?', 'It's all gone black!', 'Ouch! That was my foot!' and other similar exclamations. Then he listened to the angels telling him to 'Go, and go quickly', before God carried out his punishment on the town.

Lot told his wife to pack. He told his daughters to get ready to leave. He told the men who were going to marry his daughters to prepare for a life on the road. Everyone took him seriously, apart from the prospective sons-in-law who did what other people do in this story when they hear outrageous news. They laughed. However, by the time God had finished with the city ,they wouldn't have another side of their faces to laugh on.

Lot's family were urged out of the city by the angels. Just Lot, Mrs Lot and the two Miss Lots. As they walked through the city gates, they heard an angel shout, 'Run for your lives! Keep going and don't look back!'

Their time in the city was over. In fact, everyone's time in the city was over. New beginnings for the Lot family meant letting go of the past and moving on. There had to be no glancing over their shoulders with thoughts of, 'If only...'

A little town called Zoar was nearby. Lot's family ran there for safety, and as they got to the town walls, they heard what sounded like the biggest firework display in the world coming from behind them. It probably looked magnificent but, of

course, they would never know, because God had told them not to look. Lot's wife decided to risk a quick peek, though, thinking she could tell her family what she'd seen. Well, she *could* have told the others if, at the very moment she glanced round, she hadn't been turned into a pillar of salt. Lot had his eyes closed, and was looking forwards (if you can do that with your eyes closed – he was taking no chances though) so it wasn't until later when somebody wanted to know 'who left that woman-shaped block of salt in the gateway to the town' that what had happened to Mrs Lot became clear. It was harsh, but God had given his instructions clearly and people had to learn that when God said something he meant it. The good news was that the people of Zoar weren't short of flavouring for their vegetables and stews for months. They had a whole (Mrs) Lot of salt!

Abraham came out of his tent the next morning up on the hills, and saw far below him in the valley the smouldering ruins of not only Sodom but Gommorah as well. He thought back to his deal with God. Had Lot and his family been saved? He hoped so. If not, at least he could cancel his next trip to the zoo.

4 THE ALTAR BOY AND THE KID

There was laughter in the tents. There had been laughter before – the laughter of an old woman who thought the idea of having a baby was completely beyond imagining; a mocking, scornful, 'Come off it, who do you think you are kidding?' sort of laughter. But that wasn't the sound you could hear now. It was a mixture of excitement, happiness and joy, like waking up and finding that your birthday, Christmas, the first day of the holidays and the abolition of brussel sprouts had all arrived on the same day.

What had happened to create such hilarity? Had Abraham just told the funniest joke in the world? (That age-old favourite 'Why did the camel cross the desert?' They don't write them like that anymore.) No, it was all very simple (although Sarah might have had a different view). What had been promised all those years ago had happened! Abraham was a dad. Well, yes alright, he had been for some years, but this time it was Sarah who was the mum. The baby they had longed for was here, he was fit and healthy and he was *theirs*. No wonder they called their son 'Laughing Boy' (or 'Isaac' as it was pronounced in their language, Zac for short); *every* wonder that the birth had taken place at all.

Now, when Abraham walked around the camp at night, holding baby Isaac in his arms as he rocked him

36

to sleep, he would look up at the starlit skies and the phrase 'Father of many nations' rang round and round his head. 'Me,' he thought, 'it has all been promised to *me* and here in my hands is the proof that God keeps his promises.' At this point, God's 'kept promise' started to yell for his next feed, so that brought that bit of philosophical pondering to an end. Father of many nations? Being the father of one newborn baby at the age of 100 was challenge enough for the moment.

Heir-raising is not an easy task. At times, quite hair-raising, in fact! Things were complicated in this case by the fact that Abraham had two sons. He couldn't just assume that Isaac would inherit all his wealth and possessions. What was to stop Ishmael trying to stir things up and put in a prior claim? Ishmael might never have been promised that his children and grandchildren would be as numerous

GENESIS 21:9-21; 25:12-18

as the stars, but it was entirely possible that he would settle for leadership of Abraham's people in the short term.

Every time she saw Ishmael running through the camp, these were the kind of thoughts that ran through Sarah's head. Eventually it all got too much and she told Abraham, 'That boy has got to go! And his mother too!' But it had been Sarah's idea for him to have a son with her slave, and he had chosen to take her up on the offer. Now just because Hagar and Ishmael were a bit of an embarrassment, Abraham was being asked to send them out into the wilds where anything could happen to them ('and hopefully anything would' was what Sarah was thinking, though she kept her thoughts to herself).

Abraham did not know what to do and then God had a word. Well, several words. He told Abraham to do what Sarah wanted. Sarah would relax and be assured that Isaac really was the true heir and he (God) would take care of the rest. So it was that with just a little bread and water, Ishmael and Hagar left Abraham's campsite. Of course bread soon runs out and water doesn't last long in the desert. It wasn't long before Hagar slumped beneath a tree and closed her eyes. If Ishmael was going to die, she didn't want to see it happen.

Was it a dream or delirium brought on by the heat of the desert? Hagar wasn't sure but she could hear a voice. An angel voice telling her that she and Ishmael would survive, and that they need not worry. One day Ishmael would head up a great family of his own. When Hagar opened her eyes there was no angel, *nobody* in sight at all, but there was a well, and a well meant water and water meant staying alive.

Things went well for Hagar and Ishmael after that. Another tribe took them in. Later, Ishmael married someone from Egypt and the twelve grandsons he gave to Hagar were a bit of a bonus (on a good day).

Isaac was growing up and Abraham was growing older. He may not have thought he was going to be around to see the 'Father of Nations' bit, but he was content to believe that Isaac would see it all happen. Which explains why the next conversation he had with God was a bit of a shock. It went something like this:

Genesis 22:1–24; 23:1–20

God: Abraham.

Abe: Yes, Lord?

God: About Isaac...

Abe: Ah yes, Zac. My pride, my joy, my light, my life. Zac, in whom all my hopes for the future are invested. Zac, his mother's little helper, a delight to his father. Zac, the one who...

God: Yes, yes, yes. We've established who we're talking about. Now I want you to kill him as an offering to me.

There were no arguments, no cries of, 'Could you repeat that please? My hearing is not what it was,' no shouts of disbelief. If Abraham was shocked, stunned, dismayed or a combination of all three, he didn't let this show. Ever since he had left his home town and chosen to believe that God could be trusted, he had learned (slowly) that this was the wisest choice he could make. If this was what God wanted, then this was what would happen. Abraham would leave the consequences with him.

Next day he told Zac they were going on a journey. He took wood and two servants. (They were probably twins – if he was going to start a fire he would need a good match!) With the donkey loaded up, and farewells said to Sarah, they set off. Whether or not Abraham had told Sarah what he was going to do, we don't know. Hardly likely. Sarah, as we have seen, laughed at lots of stuff but something told Abraham that this was one thing that she was not going to find funny.

They travelled for three days, until Abraham saw the mountain where God had told him to go. Abraham and Zac left the servants. It didn't sound much to them when Abraham said, '*We* will come back,' but for Abraham it was probably the greatest statement of faith he had ever made.

Zac was a bright lad. He spotted the wood and hot coals. He knew his dad had a knife, but there was something missing from

this portable sacrifice kit and it didn't escape Zac's attention. A sacrifice had to have something to sacrifice and since they had left the donkey with the servants, he wasn't sure what they were going to use.

'Dad...' he started. Abraham tensed up. For the first and possibly the last time in history, here was a father who actually wanted his child to ask him 'Are we nearly there yet?' It would be a lot easier to deal with than anything else he might ask. But he was about to be disappointed. 'Dad, there's no sacrifice. Shouldn't we have brought something with us? A baby goat perhaps?' Abraham looked at his own kid, and there was a moment of hesitation, but his faith held firm. 'God will provide the sacrifice,' he said. There was a nagging voice at the back of his head that seemed to keep saying, 'It was God who provided Isaac,' but he did his best to ignore it.

When they had built the altar and laid the fire, Zac began to look round for God's provided sacrifice but he couldn't see anything, apart from his dad with a rope. His dad with a rope walking towards him. His dad holding out the rope – the rope which they were going to use to tie up the sacrifice. Isaac was so busy trying to figure it out, that Abraham was already pulling the knots tight before it dawned on Zac that *he* had suddenly been promoted from Assistant Stage Manager of this mountainside drama to starring role. Not that there was much chance for action – the ropes were too tight and he couldn't move.

Zac lay on top of the wood on top of the altar, saying not a word – whether because he was petrified or because he was full of the faith that seemed to be inspiring his father, I'll leave it to you to decide.

Abraham lifted the knife into the air. It flashed in the sunlight, and then it started to come down straight at Isaac. (Well, I expect it wobbled a bit – Abraham was only human after all.) Zac screwed his eyes shut. Abraham couldn't bear to watch either[5]. If *you* have your eyes closed how are you managing to read this, eh?

The knife was sharp, Zac's flesh was young and tender, and the angel shouted out just in time. Abraham froze as he heard his name being yelled across the mountainside. The angel told Abraham that he had proved his commitment to God's plans no matter what. God knew that Abraham could be trusted with the big responsibility of being the father of the faithful. A sheep bleated. It was trapped in the thorns of a nearby bush, and although Zac was not a cruel boy, he didn't waste a moment once his ropes had been cut, rushing to help his father prepare this new sacrifice. As the sheep was killed, Abraham said that he would give the mountain a new name in memory of all that had happened that day. 'Phew!', 'Close shave' and 'Near miss' were all rejected

---

[5] Ed – Even I've got my eyes closed thinking about it.

in favour of 'The Lord will provide'. He had provided
a son. He had provided the animal for sacrifice. He
would provide a land for the people who would come
after Abraham.

As they walked back home, Zac was, no
doubt, longing to ask if his dad would have
really gone through with it. But there are some
questions you *really* don't want to know the
answer to.

Once Abraham and Zac were back home, life
continued much as before. There were herds to
herd, flocks to flock, tents to repair and stories to
tell round the campfire of the land that would one

day be
theirs. But
even in well-ordered
communities, there is
sadness and grief, and sure
enough one day Sarah
stopped laughing. In fact,
she had stopped doing
anything. She was dead.
She was 127 when she
died – as they might have
said in another age, a
pretty good innings.

There was no local
cemetery, no family plot with vaults and
privately owned tombstones. It was too far to take Sarah back to
where she had come from. Besides, Abraham was convinced that
God's plan for his life was to move forwards not backwards. But his
wife needed a proper burial on land of their own, not in a
foreigner's field. The Hittites owned the land where Abraham was
camping, and there was a cave that was just the thing he was
looking for. He tried to buy it. The owner wanted to give it to him,

but Abraham wanted to say that this was his own property and he won the argument.

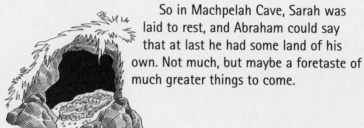

So in Machpelah Cave, Sarah was laid to rest, and Abraham could say that at last he had some land of his own. Not much, but maybe a foretaste of much greater things to come.

Now, hold on a minute, I just need to get this right. Abraham has son... God says 'Kill son as an offering'... Abraham nearly does... at the last second (and centimetre) God sends an angel to say 'Stop!', and provides a sheep... son is not killed after all.

Bit like another story that happened hundreds of years later. There was a father then, and a son, too. The son was going to be killed but at the last second, or centimetre, no one said 'Stop!'. No angel came to the rescue. The father had to watch his son die. The Bible says it like this:

'For God [he's the 'father'] loved the world so much that he gave his only Son [that's Jesus], so that everyone who believes in him may not die but have eternal life.' So God allowed what he'd stopped Abraham from doing – and he did it for everyone in the world. For me? For you? Yep – that's what he says.

5 THE END OF AN ERA

Time marched on. Well, for Abraham, because of his advanced years, it seemed to totter about with the aid of a couple of walking sticks, but there were still things to be done. Old though Abraham was, he hadn't lost his marbles (he kept them safe in a little bag under his tunic) and he knew that one son by legal means, and another by more dubious practices, did *not* amount to a family as numerous as the stars in the sky. This was just the first link in the chain. An important link, a link without which there would be no further links, but just a link nonetheless.

Which *links* us in neatly to the need for Zac to find a wife and go on 'forging links' as it were. There were plenty of women to choose from, and Zac was a good prospect – his dad had the sort of flocks that a girl's father would walk a long way to get his hands on. But Abraham didn't want any of that. He wanted a wife from his old land, a wife who would maintain a connection with all those memories of the land he and Sarah had left many years ago.

In those days, things were done differently. If Dad decided his son and heir needed a wife, Dad organised it all. He didn't stop at booking a marquee for the reception, ordering the flowers and designing the seating plan. Oh no, as far as Abraham was concerned, it was his job to find the right girl as well. Obviously he couldn't travel all the way back home at his age (even with his day-saver OAP camel-pass), so he sent one of his servants to seek out Miss Right, his 'Miss-ing Link'.

> WEDDING LIST! HMM! FIRST THING TO GET IS A BRIDE! HMMM?

The servant, plus ten camels laden with presents, set off and came to Syria to the town where Abraham's brother (Nahor) lived. There were plenty of young girls to choose from, so the servant devised a clever plan. He would wait by the well. When the girls

> NO THANKS LUV, I'VE JUST BOUGHT THIS ONE.

came, he would ask for a drink. If a girl offered to give a drink to his camels as well, he would take this as a sign that she was the one.

Rebekah was the first to arrive and, sure enough, once the servant had asked for a drink she offered to give water to the camels as well.

The servant gave her presents – rings, bracelets and assorted jewellery.

Not a bad tip for dropping a bucket down a well. Then he asked if he could have a bed for the night. No problem – Rebekah would arrange it all.

If the servant had any doubts about this being the girl for Zac, all hesitation disappeared when he discovered that her grandfather was none other than Abraham's brother, Nahor. This made Rebekah Zac's half-cousin, and there was no reason why the bells shouldn't ring from every steeple in the land. (Apart from the fact that there were no bells – or steeples come to think of it.)

Rebekah took the servant home where he told his story: the long journey, the searing heat of the days, the chill of the nights; wrestling with wild animals and beating off bandits (okay – so he exaggerated a little, but, hey, it all made for a good story); stopping at the well and asking for a drink, then discovering that he had found Abraham's family.

What a long evening that was: the surprise that Abraham was still knocking around (and knocking on); the 'I'm so sorry,' when they heard about Sarah; the interest in Isaac; and the thought that there would soon be a wedding. By the end of the evening, it was all agreed. Rebekah could go with the servant, the servant could leave all the gifts and gold behind, the camels could do what they were told and not get the hump and all would be well.

Of course, decisions taken amid the excitement of family reunions look less promising in the cold light of dawn, and come the next day the family were not sure that they were ready to let Rebekah go just yet – for a start, who was going to get the water from the well? But the servant insisted. He *had* to go back. Abraham was waiting, and he couldn't be expected to wait for ever. Rebekah was happy to leave there and then, and so they set off.

They came across Zac in south Canaan, where he was walking in the fields. Rebekah had no idea what her half-cousin looked like, but this bloke would do very nicely. Which was just as well, because before you could say 'Wilt thou take... and wilt thou also...' the two were married, and started out on the very important business of forging more links – over which we will draw a discreet tent-flap.

If Abraham had been like most old codgers, it would have been time for him to take to his tent and wait for his clogs to pop. But there was

GENESIS 25:1-11

still life in the Old Patriarch[6] yet, and before he struck camp and made for the great rest home in the sky, he married again and had six more children. They were made of strong stuff in those days, and so it was that at the age of 175, Abraham finally closed his eyes for the last time. He slipped away with a smile on his face and in the certain knowledge that what God had begun, when he brought him from his homeland all those years ago, God would complete, in God's time and in God's way...

For one hundred years, Abraham had been constantly listening to and, on at least one occasion[7], ignoring the voice of God. He had given up the security of his home and land for the vague promise of a new land for him to possess and a family to fill it.

---

[6] The Patriarchs were a bunch of really old blokes, found in the book of Genesis. You'll probably recognise their names – Adam, Noah, Arpachshad and ~~Sir Cliff Richard~~.
[7] See Hagar, Ishmael and all that.

He'd found the land, but the people filling it were certainly not *his* family – no relation at all. But during this journey, Abraham had discovered many things about God:

He could be trusted. It might have been a last minute reprieve, but he didn't allow Isaac to be killed.

You could talk things over with him. Look at the way they'd 'discussed' the Sodom situation.

God's promises were serious things. They needed to be responded to seriously. A policy of 'circumcision for the over-nineties' was not the best way to win popularity, but it was certainly a clear reminder that God meant business.

Thousands of years later, and Abraham's family fill not just one land, but the whole world – not simply his physical family, but the millions who, like Abraham, believe that the same God is at work in the world today, that he can be trusted, that you can talk to him and that he will do what he has promised. Abraham looked up at the stars and believed. Today, all over the world, people still look up and discover that the same God is waiting to lead them into new experiences of his love and purpose for their lives.

Due to the incredible adrenaline-rush quality of every page of this book, it's probably time for a breather before we travel on. So why not put this book down and, if they're out, go and look at the stars?

6 THE HAIRY HUNTER AND THE CONNIVING COOK

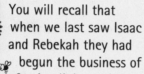

GENESIS 25:19-26

You will recall that when we last saw Isaac and Rebekah they had begun the business of forging links, and so you will be expecting to learn that soon the tinkle of tiny chains could be heard around the camp. But it wasn't to be. For twenty years, the Isaacs hoped for just one baby to keep the family line going but... nothing. Obviously, they more than just 'hoped' and when I say twenty years, there were of course the occasional breaks to feed the flocks, cook the dinner and visit the relatives. But the gist of the matter was that Zac was in the same situation as his dad had been all those years before: the promise of a huge dynasty but not even the glimmerings of a suspicion of a twinkle in his eye.

'OH! NOT EVEN A TWINKLE!'

Zac talked to God about it. God listened. Rebekah became pregnant and grew larger and rounder. Just when the rumour began that she might be giving birth to the whole family at once, it occurred to some of the brighter members of the tribe that she might be having twins. Certainly Rebekah could feel the babies inside her struggling and fighting. It all seemed very unusual, until God explained what would happen to her two children.

'Two sons. Two nations. The younger leads. The older serves.'

All she had wanted was a baby. Now according to God, she was going to be the incubation chamber for the *Dis*-United Nations. It was all very confusing. If only she had just dropped the bucket down the well all those years ago! But it was too late to go back now.

Sure enough, Rebekah had twins. As custom stated, the first-born would have the right to two-thirds of his father's land and property. Heir by birth and hairy by nature, as it turned out. He was covered at birth with fine red hair. So, with a cruelty that afflicts many parents when naming their offspring, they called him 'Hairy', or as they spelled it – 'Esau'. (I once knew a Mr and Mrs Christmas who called their first son Mary, but that's another story...)

The second child followed the first swiftly. In fact, he appeared, hanging on to his brother's heel. His name became 'Jacob' which in Zac's language sounded a bit like the word for 'heel'. Now you might not think these are the best names to give your children to assure them of your love and concern for their well-being, but in the second son's case, as we shall see, 'Heel' might have been just the right name for him.

How could two children, born at the same time, from the same parents, be so different? How often have families asked themselves that over the centuries. Esau was the hunter. He loved the outdoors, and was never happier than when he had a dead animal slung over his shoulders, the smell of freshly-shed blood in his nostrils and the dying screams of his prey ringing in his ears. Still, it takes all sorts. Jake on the other hand was more your 'stay at home' type. He'd go out into the fields and count up the sheep during the day. But he would never

GENESIS 25:27-34

wander far from the campsite. He was happiest with a pot boiling away on the fire and a stack of herbs, spices and assorted ingredients with which to create something a little special for the evening meal. If it couldn't be stewed, sautéed, grilled, baked, roasted or steamed, then Jake didn't really want to know.

He was busy adding the finishing touches to a little something in the home-made, purely-organic, soup department, when Esau arrived back from his latest hunting trip. As he approached the camp, he could smell

54

the stew and his mouth began to water. Esau dumped his catch and went to find Jake. 'Food, Jake, I've got to have food! Feed me!' he shouted as he rushed up to the kitchens. 'Nearly ready,' said Jake, 'just give it a little more time to bring out the flavours.'

'I need to eat NOW!' yelled Esau, 'I'm starving.' Jake looked into his brother's eyes. He could see the longing in them, the hunger and desperation that comes from being out hunting for three days longer than your food supplies last... and an idea began to form in his mind.

'How hungry *are* you?' he asked dipping a ladle in the pot and wafting it under his brother's nose.

'Look, what do you want?' Esau asked. 'I'll give you anything.'

'Anything?'

'Yes, just give me some food.'

'Well,' said Jake, 'what have you got that I could possibly want? Your collection of arrows smeared with the blood of dead animals? No, I don't think so. Your range of hair applications and conditioners? Very necessary in your case, but not a lot of use to me.' Jake paused and then added, almost as if it were an afterthought, 'Of course, there is always your birthright.'

The birthright. Esau's right as first-born not simply to inherit most of his father's goods and wealth, but even more importantly, the right to be head of the family, leader of the pack, head honcho, chief of the tribe. But right now that all seemed like pie in the sky and Esau wanted steak-on-a-plate and quickly-mate (actually it was red lentil soup, but if you think I've time to sit here and find a rhyme for lentils... think again!).

'Agreed,' yelled Esau, 'now just give me the food!'

Jake handed over a bowl of the soup and, because he was in a happy mood (after all he had just become the main inheritor of his father's estate, which in the world of catering counts as a 'good tip'), he let Esau have some bread as well to mop up the juices. Although, as we have just seen, when it came to mopping up *Jake* was the expert.

Esau ate and drank and Jake was merry. They both slept well that night. One full of what he *had* received, the other full of thoughts of what he *would* receive... and he was truly thankful.

Jake couldn't keep the news to himself. He told his mum who beamed with delight. It's always dangerous in families to have favourites, but Rebekah had never made any secret of the fact that she had

GENESIS 26:34–28:5

more time for Jake than for Esau. In her mind, it was only right that he should inherit. He had been the one who stayed at home, and who had been there when she needed him. He was sophisticated and well-mannered, unlike his brother who could find

nothing better to do than chase around after animals, and leave carcasses all over the place (no matter how much you scrub, there are some stains you just can't get out of your best camelskin rug).

Esau didn't help matters by going off and marrying 'outside' the family. The Hittites were OK as neighbours, and handy when you needed to negotiate some grazing rights, but you didn't really want to be related to them. To make

it worse, Esau didn't just go for one foreign wife – he had two – and Rebekah just knew that this was going to mean trouble. She began to think carefully about the future. How could she ensure that Jake got the best of the family deals and that her daughters-in-law were kept as much out of the picture as possible? A cunning plan began to form in her mind. A plan that would make Jake's quick deal on the 'soup-for-birthright' front look like he was only just practising.

Isaac was getting older, his eyesight had gone and the whisper around the campsite was that it 'would only be a matter of time...' He had been the first link in the chain, but there was one more thing he had to do before he passed away. He wanted to give a blessing. The father's blessing in a family was important. There was something sacred about the words which would contain promises and hopes that God would honour. It wasn't just a few thoughts to comfort the children in their time of grief. It was about lives being shaped for the future.

While he still could, Isaac called Esau and asked him to prepare some food that he had caught himself. Isaac promised that as they ate, he would give his first-born son his blessing. As so often in God's dealing with people, food forms a central focus for all that is being done. Thousands of years after Isaac had shared this final meal with Esau, a carpenter from Nazareth would have a last meal with his friends and the promises made then have been shared at meals around the world ever since.

As Esau set off to hunt down their dinner, Rebekah put the plan that had been running around her head for so long into operation. She called Jake and gave her instructions. She wanted two goats to cook. With enough herbs and spices, she reckoned she could disguise the flavour so that Isaac would believe he was eating wild boar. His eyesight was so bad he'd not be able to tell by looking. If Jake could serve it up to him before Esau got back, then *he* would get the blessing of his father.

There was a problem. The taste of the food could be disguised, but his dad only had to touch Jake and he would know something was afoot. Jake was smooth and clean cut. Esau, on the other hand, was a stranger to comb, razor and good grooming. How were they going to get away with it? But Rebekah had thought of everything. Stewed goat meant a spare goat skin

HE'S GOING TO COOK US! THAT REALLY GETS MY GOAT!

AW, YOU'RE KIDDING!

lying around. Rough, hairy, smelly skin just like Esau's (not to be too delicate about it). If Jake dressed himself in the skin, then the plan might just work.

A short time later, Jake went into his father's tent, calling out, 'I'm here, Dad. It's me, Esau. I have brought you your supper.' Isaac was amazed. Surely there hadn't been time to hunt, kill, prepare and cook an animal? How could Esau have been so quick? 'God was good to me,' came the answer, after Isaac had voiced the question. That God was good to Jake was further proved by the fact that he didn't strike him dead on the spot for such a blatant lie!

Something was puzzling Isaac about all this, but he couldn't quite put his finger on it. He did put his finger on two hairy arms and a hair neck, but the little niggle in the back of his head wouldn't go away. It was tough getting old. Everything was so confusing. Here was someone who *felt* like Esau, but *sounded* like Jake. It was the smell that finally convinced him.

Nobody who wasn't Esau would choose to smell like that, surely? And so the meal was eaten and Isaac took Jake, kissed him and offered him his blessing and God's promises:

'God's blessing fall upon you.
May your fields flourish and your grapes grow greatly,
May you be served by your brother,
May he respect no other.
Those you curse will fare worse,
Those you bless meet with success.'

Jake left the tent, gave his mother the thumbs-up and went for a very long soak in a lotion-filled bath.

Meanwhile Esau had returned and prepared the food his father wanted. 'I'm here, Dad. It's me, Esau. I have brought you your supper,' he said, as he went into his father's tent. Isaac sat up and felt very confused. What was going on? His memory was getting bad but this was ridiculous! If this was Esau, who had he just given his blessing to? A blessing which, given freely could not be taken back. Slowly it sank in. Jake had tricked his father and Esau was, quite literally, the poor relation. To be cheated out of your inheritance once could be considered a misfortune. When it happens twice, you can't help but think that you have lost the plot somewhere.

Esau was desperate. 'Is there nothing you can promise me?' he pleaded with Isaac. His father ran things through in his head. He had promised Jake that he would have all the crops, the blessing of a good harvest and rule over his brother. What was left? Isaac thought long and hard and then said:

'True, the fields are his.
Your home shall be far from here.
You shall fight to stay alive
But there is news to bring you cheer.
Your brother shall rule your life,
His control feeling like a noose,
But it will not be for ever –
One day you shall break loose!'

'Well,' thought Esau, 'it's better than nothing I suppose. But not as good as killing Jacob is going to be. If he thinks he can get away with this, then he'd better watch out. When I get hold of him I'll...'
Esau lost himself in a dream of all the terrible things that he could do to his conniving, low-life brother but nothing seemed good enough. Or should that be awful enough? They say 'revenge is a dish best served cold'. Esau didn't know a lot about serving dishes, but he was certain that Jake was going to get his just desserts.

7 HAIR TODAY GONE TOMORROW

WOT'S WRONG WITH BEING PINK AND WRINKLY?

GENESIS 28:10-22

Rebekah knew that there would be trouble. Esau had a short fuse and Jake couldn't hide in the bath for ever. Apart from anything else, he'd go all pink and wrinkly and who wants to marry a pink wrinkly (apart from another pink wrinkly that is)? She needed to get Jake away from the family, and at the same time she wanted to make sure he married in the family (very confusing, I know, but once you start plotting you have to cover all your options). A light bulb appeared above her head – the universal sign that a good idea had just been born. (What they made of it in the days before Edison[8], I have no idea.) Let's just say that Rebekah was in the position of staring at two birds with only one stone in her hand, when she suddenly realised how she could kill them both. All she had to do was persuade Isaac that Jake needed to go to live with her brother Laban's family. Telling him that Jake was sure to meet a nice girl of his own sort,

WOW! LOOK AT THAT!

MAN! IT'S BEAUTIFUL!

---

[8] If you're not sure who he is, don't ask me, ask a science teacher.

was just the way to swing it – especially as Esau had recently married a third foreign woman just to spite his family. Of course with Uncle Laban, Jake would be safe from Esau and his plans for revenge.

It all fitted together perfectly. Rebekah told Jake what he had to do and that day he set off for Haran. It was a long journey, and there was plenty of time to think. Yes, he'd got the money and the property. Yes, there was the promise from his father of all that would be his. But there was a little part of him that niggled away and a voice that seemed to simply repeat the word 'Cheat' round and round his head. What's the point of gaining the world and losing your soul as someone was to observe many years later? How could God be interested in a deceitful double-crosser like Jake? Even if his family did fill the earth as Abraham had been promised, was he destined to be the family member who was never discussed at special occasions? The one who, if his name was mentioned, would be consigned to oblivion with sharp intakes of breath, tut-tuts and a hasty change of subject?

With these thoughts racing through his mind, he stopped for the night. He'd left in a hurry, so there was no feather-filled duvet or pillows to help keep him warm and comfy while he slept. No, he had to make do with wrapping his cloak round a bit tighter and putting his head on a stone and 'rock'ing himself to sleep. As he slept he dreamed.

There was a ladder. It stretched from earth to heaven and angels were constantly wandering up and down, busy doing God's work. As Jake watched in his dream, he heard God speak to him. 'This is your land – I will give it to you. You are on the run, you have cheated and lied, your brother hates you. All this is true. But my work goes on without ceasing, just as these angels never cease from moving up and down. I am not going to abandon you, Jacob, even though your thoughts are often far from me. You are not the first disobedient person I have worked with, and you won't be the last. Changing lives and bringing the good out of the bad – even when the bad is as bad as you – is what I'm good at. I will do what I have promised and you will be part of it.'

Jake woke sweating and trembling – God was with him in this place. God knew all about Jake's life and sins and he was *still* with him. For the first time in his life, Jake had the unusual experience of being humbled. Suddenly he knew that he wasn't the most important person in the universe. He had a responsibility to someone much greater than himself.

Before he continued his journey, he worshipped God and, setting upright the rock he had been using as a pillow, he made a promise to God. 'God, you met me in this place, so I rename it the "House of God". Let us travel together and, if you allow, I will come back to this place and a tenth of all that I receive in the future will be yours.'

So Jake travelled on. But he didn't feel as though he was running from the mess of his life any more, but walking with purpose towards the future that was to be his, with God by his side.

The journey had been long and the lack of a good map and signposts hadn't helped. By the time Jacob reached the well he had seen from some distance away, he was tired (well tired!). Some shepherds were at the well, waiting for other shepherds to come before they began watering their sheep. To

while away the time, Jake made conversation. 'I don't suppose any of you know a man called Laban?' he asked. 'Know him?'

laughed one of the shepherds, 'Of course we know him! That's his flock of sheep coming this way.' He pointed into the distance, and Jake saw someone coming along with more sheep. Jake had never met his Uncle Laban, but he suspected that the rather attractive young woman who arrived at the well with the sheep was not him.

Rachel (the young woman with the sheep) was gathering her sheep together when suddenly a complete stranger rushed up to her and kissed her. Now that kind of thing doesn't happen every day of the week. If it did, shepherding might be a more popular career choice. 'I'm your cousin,' said the stranger – which of course makes

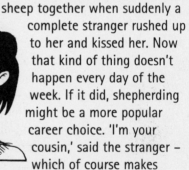

rushing up to women and kissing them perfectly OK in any culture (NOT!). 'Oh great! I'll go and tell my dad,' said Rachel (meaning: I think I'll feel a bit safer if my dad's with me, strange-but-curiously-attractive-gentleman-who-has-appeared-from-nowhere).

It had been at least sixty years since Laban had seen his sister Rebekah leave with Abraham's servant to marry Isaac. (I do hope you are keeping up with all these people... there may be a short test at the end.) Now here was his nephew with news of all the family. He was already thinking of the feasting there would be, the telling of stories and the inevitable anecdotes that begin with 'I remember when...' At family gatherings, this is usually the best time to slip out quietly and find something more exciting to do, such as sorting out your sock drawer, arranging your CDs into alphabetical order, or colouring in all the blank squares on a crossword puzzle. So, if you want to slip off for a bit now's your chance... we'll wait.

A month has passed by. (You were gone longer than you thought, weren't you? Still, no time spent arranging spaghetti according to length is ever wasted really, is it?) Four long weeks since Jake had kissed Rachel when she wasn't looking. He hadn't kissed her since (but she was looking all the time). Jake had begun to settle down with his new family, and was proving invaluable in helping Uncle Laban cosset his cattle and fettle his flock (farming terms – don't worry about it). He was proving *so* useful that Laban began to wonder how on earth he had managed before Jake arrived, and the thought that he might suddenly decide it was time to go back home worried him. Laban was no mean[9] businessman, and the four weeks' unpaid work he had got out of Jake had suited him very well. But even Laban knew that it couldn't go on for ever. He was going to have to offer some kind of reward in exchange for Jake's continued labour. So it was that he asked Jake to name his price.

LABAN

JACOB

RACHEL

---

[9] Mean as in shrewd, not mean as in mean – he *was* a bit stingy, as we'll soon find out.

Jake didn't want money. The lack of Megastores in this part of the wilderness was shocking, and it was all very well burying your money under a rock for a rainy day, but even if it rained (which it didn't very often) you couldn't be sure that you would remember which rock your money was under.

No, Jake had his eyes on a higher prize. He knew when she first stepped up to the well on that hot day a month earlier that Rachel was more than a mirage: she was the girl of his dreams. She had an older sister, Leah, who was very pleasant but lacked a certain... oh, I don't know, 'je ne sais quoi'. No, Rachel was the one for him. He thought marrying Rachel might be a lot to ask in return for a few weeks' work, and the custom in those days was to offer the bride's family money in return for her hand (and the rest of her) in marriage.

Jake didn't have any money, but he thought he would be able to do a deal with Laban. 'I'll work for you for seven years if you let me marry Rachel,' he offered. 'Done,' said Laban. (And Jake would be – as we shall see.)

8 HOW THE TRICKY TRICKSTER GOT TRICKED

Seven years went by. A lifetime to some (especially if you're only seven) but to Jake the time flew by. If he ever grew weary or impatient, he only had to glance over to where Rachel was working to know that it would all be worthwhile. For her, he would have composed symphonies, trekked across deserts with only a camel for company, or let himself be buried in treacle and left to the mercy of the ants (he was funny like that) – but you get the idea. He was IN LURRRRVE!

The time had come for Laban to keep his part of the bargain. So he organised a wedding party and

brought his daughter – dressed in bridal splendour with enough veils, trains, flounces and gussets to make your eyes water – to Jake. They shook on the deal, and that night Jake took Laban's daughter to his tent without further ado. He had waited seven years... and he was going to wait no longer (if you see what I mean).

The next morning, sunlight flooded the tent. Jake turned over to his new bride and stared into the eyes of... Leah.

His yells could be heard far and wide. He stormed out of the tent shouting for Laban. He stormed back in, put some clothes on, and started yelling all over again. Jake had played some pretty rotten tricks on Esau in the past, but being palmed off with the wrong sister was something to which even he would never have stooped. Well probably not... OK, if there had been some advantage to be gained, he might have thought about it... but that's not the point. The point is that Laban had tricked Jacob, and Jake didn't like it one little bit.

Laban seemed surprised there was a problem. 'Surely you know our customs? The oldest daughter must always marry first. You are not suggesting that I should have done something else, surely? Look the wedding feast is still going on. When it's over, we can discuss other possibilities.'

Jake had made his promise to God, and he had been trying to behave better since leaving his family. With a forced smile on his face, he took his hands from round Laban's neck and went back to the feasting. Wedding parties lasted for a week in that neck of the woods (which probably explains why the wine ran out at a wedding Jesus went to once), and Jake tried hard to enjoy himself. Leah wasn't bad. In fact she was quite presentable. She had lovely eyes... but she wasn't Rachel. All kinds of thoughts whirled around his head, as he tried to think of a way of resolving the difficulty. However, any ideas he did have were lost due to

his anger over how devious Laban had been.

'What an excuse – sticking to the customs of his land,' thought Jake. 'I suppose he only does that when it suits... just a minute!' Jake had the answer. The customs of the land not only had rules about elder daughters, but also about a man's right to have more than one wife. That was the answer – he would marry Rachel as well!

LOOK! IT'S BACK!

M-M-MUST TOUCH IT!

IT LOOKS SO HOT!

Sure enough, at the end of the wedding week, just as the caterers were beginning to pack up, another party began – this time to celebrate the wedding of Rachel and Jake. He had agreed to work a further seven years as the bridal price, but this time he got to marry the girl first.

It was obvious to anyone who passed by Laban's camp that Jake was in love with Rachel. It was most obvious to Leah, who after all the excitement of her wedding, now had to take second place to her little sister. It's not that Jake was unkind, but there was definitely a difference between the way the two women were treated. However, as the years went by, Leah had something that Rachel didn't have... children. Four, in fact, in a very short space of time.

Now you might have thought that having to make your way through lines of nappies, compete with the cries of little ones whenever you wanted to make yourself heard and take your turn on the babysitting rota would have given you an insight into being a mother that would have put you off for life. But not Rachel – not any woman in those days. Having children was what you got married for. The more children, the more sure you could be that the family name would be carried on. Now, clearly, Jake and Leah were doing all they could to keep the family name going, but that didn't help Rachel. She felt like a failure as a wife. It wasn't fair, and if Jake really loved her he would give her babies too. It all came out one day in a torrent of anger and bitterness, which is often when people say and do the things they will regret later.

Rachel had a servant girl called Bilhah. In the same way that Sarah let Abraham sleep with Hagar, now Rachel gave Bilhah to Jake.

Bilhah had two babies. Leah, not to be outdone, gave *her* servant girl, Zilpah, to Jake and she had two sons as well. That makes eight so far – all boys – and time to call it a day surely? But no, Leah went on to have three more children, one of which was a girl which made passing on the hand-me downs a bit tricky.

If this is all getting a bit confusing, here's a quick guide to who is married to who and which child belongs to who (to whom?).[10]

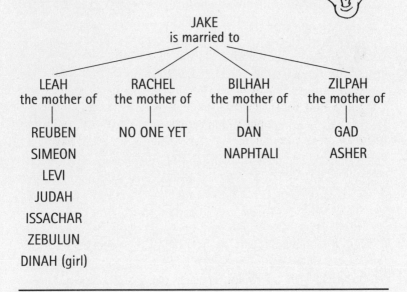

JAKE
is married to

LEAH the mother of	RACHEL the mother of	BILHAH the mother of	ZILPAH the mother of
REUBEN	NO ONE YET	DAN	GAD
SIMEON		NAPHTALI	ASHER
LEVI			
JUDAH			
ISSACHAR			
ZEBULUN			
DINAH (girl)			

---

[10] Read the last bit of this sentence quickly and you'll do a good impression of an owl.

Eventually, however, Rachel had her prayers answered, and she too gave birth to a son. 'My shame has been taken away, my joy has been added to,' said Rachel as she brought out her child to show to the family. He was to be called Joseph, and it will come as no surprise to learn that his name sounds a bit like 'taken away' and 'added to'. Very clever, these Hebrews, when it comes to names.

Jake, so far the father of eleven sons (and one daughter), had really taken the business of populating future generations to heart. I don't know that it had ever really been God's intention that he should try to do the task all by himself, but nobody could deny that he'd given it a good go!

Of course, the deal had been numerous family generations and a land of their own. Well, the generation potential was coming along nicely but Jake was back in Haran which was where his grandfather, Abraham, had been told to leave many years ago. He knew he had to go back to Canaan – but he also had this agreement to work with Laban. It was time to renegotiate the contract.

Laban didn't want to let a good worker go. He had his daughters and grandchildren around him, and a son-in-law who seemed to have a knack of making things flourish (and we're not just talking about babies here).

Laban had been doing all right before Jake came on the scene, but recently his herds and flocks had grown beyond his wildest dreams. He would be a fool to let Jake go. Jake could see that moving on was going to be tricky, but he began to make his plans.

When the time did come to leave, he would need his own herds and flocks to take with him – he wasn't going back to Canaan empty-handed – so he began to work out a plan with Laban. The deal was that Jake could have all the spotted, speckled and black sheep or goats and Laban would have all the rest. Since most of Laban's sheep were

white this didn't seem too hard a loss to bear. Of course, they would have to be kept separate and Jake was happy about that. Once the flocks had been divided, it was time to engage in a little local superstition.

There was a belief in those parts that whatever animals were looking at during the mating season (try reading this next bit with your eyes half closed if it's a bit embarrassing) would be reflected in their offspring. Jake thought it was worth a try, and so all around where the flocks were kept, he set

up poles that were striped and speckled. Whether it was local magic or God looking after Jake, you have to decide. Sure enough when lambing time came the lambs were spotted and so, according to the deal, belonged to Jake not Laban. Jake may have left behind those days of cheating and lying, but he clearly still had a devious streak inside him (it was definitely a streak, not spots or speckles). Slowly there was a change in fortunes. Jake's flocks got larger and larger, and once he had sold and traded a few, he was surrounded by camels, donkeys and slaves – and they were all his.

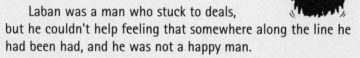

Laban was a man who stuck to deals, but he couldn't help feeling that somewhere along the line he had been had, and he was not a happy man.

9 A SPOT OF BOTHER

GENESIS
31:1-55

Things had started to change. Jake would walk into a tent and Laban would walk out. His brothers-in-law would be talking in corners, and suddenly go quiet when Jake walked in. There was definitely a bad atmosphere, and Jake couldn't help feeling that somehow he was behind it all. Clearly his success had not been universally, or even locally, popular. Laban's sons could make things difficult for him, but

he was not afraid. God had got him this far, and Jake was certain that he would not leave him. He called Rachel and Leah to a meeting and told them they were leaving. If he'd expected cries of, 'Oh no, I can't leave Daddy!' and, 'It's a very bad time for the children to be changing schools!' he was surprised. Rachel and Leah had also been ignored by their father. They could see that if they stayed around, Laban would find some way of getting back all Jake's possessions. It was becoming increasingly obvious that the only thing Laban cared about was the growth and success of 'Laban and Sons'.

Jake and his family (families?) prepared to leave. Now you might be wondering, 'How do you pack up four wives, twelve children, camels, goats,

donkeys, sheep, tents, household possessions and several boxes of stuff-that-you-haven't-used-for-years-but-might-come-in-useful-some-day without letting everyone else know what is going on?' Well, farming people often moved around to better grazing

areas, or new winter quarters, and they were always looking for new spots where the grass was greener. When Jake, wives, children, etc, etc, moved off, everyone assumed that this was just another of those times. It was only when there was no news of where they had settled that Laban began to suspect that all was not as it seemed.

For seven days, Laban chased after Jake, and when he caught up with him, he demanded an explanation.

'You tricked me!' he yelled at Jake.

'You tricked me first,' came back the answer.

'I would have let you go.'

'Not without me paying the price first, like I've had to pay for everything else over the last twenty years.'

'But look at how well you've done!'

'Because I've worked hard!'

'But there was no need to take my possessions.'

'They're not yours, they're all mine – we had a deal.'

'The household gods weren't yours.'

'Look everything here is... Sorry, what did you say? I thought you said "household gods".'

'I did.'

'What household gods?'

Which, dear reader, may be the very question you are asking. In the rush to get Jake away from Laban, I forgot to mention that Rachel had taken the statues that Laban and his family worshipped. She, in turn, had forgotten to tell Jake. Which makes what happens next doubly ironic.

'I haven't got your gods,' insisted Jacob. 'My God is good enough for me. Have a look, and if you find them, you can kill whoever stole them!'

Rachel shifted uncomfortably. This wasn't just because of the thought of her possible impending doom, but also because she'd hidden the gods under her saddle, and the pointy bits kept jabbing into her. Not nice. Of course, while she stayed sitting, Laban was not going to find them. Given a choice between a painful bottom and a painful death, Rachel knew which one she would choose every time.

Laban had to give in. There was nothing he could do to get Jake and the family back. But there was one thing he could try though. He suggested an agreement between himself and his son-in-law that would ensure that each kept to his own land. He wasn't going to go chasing around after Jake any more, but he didn't want Jake returning with even more men in the future to try and take over his land. He made a pile of stones, and together they agreed that this was the boundary, and in future each of them would keep to their own end of the playing fields. It seemed a good idea to Jake and so the agreement was made.

The next day, Laban said his farewells and left. Rachel got up off her saddle and went in search of some soothing ointment, and Jake gathered everyone together for the next stage of the journey. If he'd thought that Laban might have caused trouble, there was somebody back at home who had been nursing a grievance for twenty years...

GENESIS
32:1 – 33:20

It was going to be a long time before someone uttered the words 'Better jaw-jaw than war-war'[11]. These were words that could have been written by Jake as he considered the best way of being reunited with his twin

---

[11] Translation: when trying to resolve your differences with someone, it's far better to talk things through than to use violence.

80

brother. He had tried running (and
had done very nicely, thank you) but
now it was time to face the music.

He sent messengers ahead of
him to Esau's camp, asking to be
treated kindly – well, anything was
worth a try. The messengers returned
(that was I suppose a good sign, as Esau could have just killed
them on the spot) with a message (it goes with the job) – Esau
was coming to find Jake and he had four hundred men with him
(not such a good sign). Jake suspected he was not coming to
swap Christmas presents and family snapshots. He needed to do
some thinking and quick. But first he did some praying. It was
quite a long and detailed prayer but can, I feel, be summed up
concisely and succinctly with the simple word:

HELP!

Through the night, Jake made his preparations. He went
through his flocks choosing the best as gifts for Esau. Sheep,
goats, donkeys, camels – hundreds of
them. He suspected that they might not
compensate for all that he had
cheated Esau out of years
before, but he'd still give
it a go. At the same time,
he split his men and
family into two groups: not
so much a case of 'divide
and conquer' as 'divide and

survive'. He sent his servants off with the gifts and moved his wives and children to a place of safety. He had done all he could do. Now it was up to God.

Jake didn't sleep much that night, partly because he had things on his mind: the promises God had made; the terrible deception Jake had carried out; twenty years in exile and an angry brother; the prospect of his own land and descendants that would cover the earth; his selfishness which had ruled so much of his life. Here he was, wealthy beyond his dreams, with so much promised to him – and he was scared.

As he sat and thought all these things through, over and over, he actually began struggling with someone – fighting with God to understand how all that had been promised could really come about through someone like him. 'Stony ground, Lord, on which to build a nation,' he cried. 'My ground, my choice,' came back the voice of God. Jake fell to the ground crying, 'Let it happen,  Lord. Bless me.' Jake heard the voice of God assure him that it would all be as he said. 'This is a new start, Jacob, and to go with it you shall have a new name. You who have struggled with God will be known as "God struggler – Israel".'

The fighting was over. Jake was alone, and his hip was in agony. The battle had been real – he had the injury to prove it. Jake was filled with a sense of wonder, and remembered the dream all those years before with the angels and the ladder. God was still with him. And if God was with him, what could Esau and four hundred men do to him? He walked out to greet the dawn and his destiny.

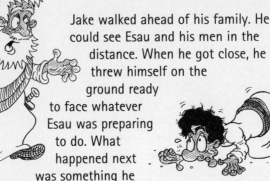

Jake walked ahead of his family. He could see Esau and his men in the distance. When he got close, he threw himself on the ground ready to face whatever Esau was preparing to do. What happened next was something he wasn't prepared for...

Esau ran to Jacob, pulled him to his feet and hugged him. Jake waited for the knife in the back but it never came. Instead, there were tears and laughter and hairy hugs. What could have been a war turned into a party!

Esau met Jake's family and gave the gifts of sheep and camels and all back to Jake. 'I have plenty,' he said. 'God has been good to me. I don't need your gifts, but I do need your friendship.' It was almost too much to bear. Jacob had taken everything from Esau – yet here was Esau offering forgiveness, friendship and a new start. Jake had brought treasures back from Haran, but nothing compared to this – the opportunity to start again.

GENESIS
35:1-21

To add to the joy, Rachel discovered she was to have another baby. But life is not all sunshine and family reunions. True, the baby was born, but the birth was difficult and Rachel died. Jacob was heartbroken, and baby Benjamin joined his older brother,

Joseph, as the reminder to Jacob in his old age of the great love of his life, Rachel.

Jacob came back to Bethel. The stone he had used as a pillow was still there. He had everyone take out any idols or statues that represented foreign gods, which he buried, and together his people committed themselves to being a people of the one true God who keeps his word and blesses his people.

And father Isaac was still alive. In his final years, Isaac was able to enjoy his family growing up. He had been an only child, who had two children, and now here was Jacob with twelve sons and a daughter and Esau with his five sons. Eighteen grandchildren. Now, if they all had, say six children and the great-grandchildren had six children, that would be... well, an awfully big family. Isaac died knowing that it was happening – God's promise was beginning to become a reality.

It had been a long time ago when God had first told Abram that he would have more family members than he could count. Well, they hadn't got to that stage yet, but they had made a good start.

It was strange really. If God had wanted a nation full of loving, holy people why didn't he just create them? And if you are going to use people to work out your plans, why use people who lie, cheat, argue and generally get it wrong? If I were God, I would have done it all very differently. Oh yes, only the best need apply, and if you didn't stick to the rules then you'd be shown the door pretty sharpish. Yes indeedy, there would be no room for slackers, weaklings or generally mixed-up, tend-to-get-it-wrong type people in my grand plan.

Although, come to think of it, if someone made up rules like that, it would mean there would be no, er, no room for me. And I expect if you were to put this book down for a moment and think about your own life there would be no space for you either. Scary.

Perhaps, on second thoughts, God's way is better. Like most people (Jacob, for example) it has taken me a little while to work this out. Still, now that we have seen that God likes to use the most unlikely of people, I don't suppose we will forget again, just like Jacob... well, actually, not just like Jacob.

Trust God – his ways are best – things work out, even if we can't see how. All these thoughts were running round Jacob's head as he buried Isaac, but they didn't stay there for long...

10 DAYDREAM BELIEVER

GENESIS 37:1-36

'Never have favourites!' It ought to be painted on the walls of every maternity ward and printed as a public health warning on the bottom of every birth certificate. If you are going to have children, you can't start loving one more than another... as Jacob found out.

Joseph was the son of Jacob's beloved wife Rachel, and although the other boys were useful for looking after the sheep and stuff, there was no one quite like Joe. Jacob pampered him – he rewarded him for sneaking on his brothers and gave him clothes that made all the others feel shabby and tatty. Mind you, they were. It's tough living out in the desert, but they didn't need this arrogant adolescent swanning around and making them feel bad. Jake would hear no bad word against him, though – Joe was his own little ray of sunshine. But the weather was about to change...

The brothers would have coped, just about, if it hadn't been for the dreams. There is, of course, only one thing more boring than someone telling you about their dreams and

that is someone showing you their holiday snaps. Well, given the absence of cameras in Canaan, it was Joe who attempted to bore-for-the-nation when one morning over breakfast he stood on the kitchen table and shouted, 'Guess what?'.

Nobody guessed. Nobody even asked what he was talking about, because they knew he was going to tell them anyway. Which he did.

Joe talked about his dreams – of harvest fields waving in the sun, and corn stacks bowing down before a bundle of wheat. There were tales of stars and the sun and moon gathering around Joe and bowing low. It was the *bowing* that did it.

The rest of the dreams were just symptomatic of a disturbed mind, they thought. But if he was seriously

suggesting that his brothers, who thought it was only fair to remind him that they were all bigger than him (apart from Benjamin... but he was growing up fast), were going to be bowing down to him, then he had better think again.

Even his father was shocked. He was the family leader and he didn't bow down to anybody (mind you, these days that was mainly because of the arthritis). However, despite Jake's misgivings, it wasn't quite enough to stop him thinking of Joe as his blue-eyed boy, and he couldn't help wondering if there was something in it after all. As for Joe's brothers, it will come as no surprise to say that they reacted a little differently. They were cross, put out, annoyed, enraged, aggravated, cheesed off and fuming – to put it in words of one syllable: THEY WERE NOT HAPPY BUNNIES (OK, I cheated on the last two words... HAPP BUNS?... anyway, I'm sure you get the idea) and their opportunity soon came to turn his dreams into a nightmare.

'WE'RE NOT HAPPY BUNNIES!'

It was some weeks later, when the brothers were out looking after the sheep over Dothan way, that Jacob sent Joe out to check that everything was going well. As it turned out, before the day was over, Joe would find himself *down* a well, but we'll come to that in due course. He set off to find his brothers and he was still quite a way off when they saw him in the distance. When ten brothers start speaking all at once, it can get a bit confusing, but if we extract the different voices, it sounded something like this...

HE WANTS PUTTING TO SLEEP PERMANENTLY!

YEAH! HE CAN DREAM AS MUCH AS HE LIKES THEN!

HERE COMES DADDY'S LITTLE DREAMER!

This last voice was Reuben's. As the eldest, he felt that he had a certain responsibility, and you couldn't go around bumping off your half-brother just because he got up your nose. On the other hand, Joe *was* a bit of a pain... so, Reuben reached a compromise. They wouldn't finish him off, just rough him up a bit and drop him down a well to scare him – a dry well, of course. They didn't want him to drown. Of course if there *was* water at the bottom – that would be too bad.

When Joe got to them, he scarcely had time to say, 'Hello, how are you? Can I tell you about last night's dream?' when they had ripped his coat off him and he was down the well.

The brothers were eating their dinner and trying to ignore the cries of, 'Hey, guys! Can I get out now? A joke's a joke... Daddy won't like it when I tell him what you've done... fellas... hello... hello?' when they became aware that they were not alone. It wasn't a new *sound* – more a new *smell*. The smell came from the camels, and the camels came from Gilead and they were on their way to Egypt. They were loaded down with all the goods of their Ishmaelite[12] owners who

---

[12] These were descendants of Ishmael, a character we met a few pages back.

were expecting to make some easy money down among the Pyramids.

Judah had an idea – Reuben was right, they shouldn't kill Joe. Of course not, especially as if they sold him they would gain some silver, get rid of Joe, and would have the whole journey back to Canaan to think of a story to convince their father that he was gone for good.

So the brothers dragged Joe up from the well, very glad of the fact that they had exercised some kind of self-control moments before. After a little haggling (it's traditional and the Ishmaelites expected it) they 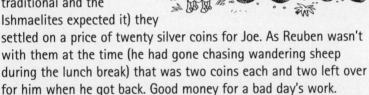 settled on a price of twenty silver coins for Joe. As Reuben wasn't with them at the time (he had gone chasing wandering sheep during the lunch break) that was two coins each and two left over for him when he got back. Good money for a bad day's work.

They were so busy counting it out, they didn't see Joe being tied up and thrust over the back of one of the camels, along with all the other goods the Ishmaelites wanted to sell in Egypt. Riding along with his nose inches away from the back-end of a camel left Joe plenty of time to think (and plenty of opportunity to practise his breath-holding exercises). How had he ended up like this? What would his dad say? What were his brothers doing now?

What his brothers were doing was working out what they were going to tell Reuben. He was quite observant, and if he went back to the well to rescue Joe, he was bound to notice someone (someone called Joe) was missing. I don't know if he got his share of the money, but I do know that he didn't split on the rest of his brothers and together they came up with a story to tell their dad.

They killed a goat and smeared its blood all over Joe's coat. When they returned home, they showed their dad the goat-dyed coat with cries of, 'We found this... We think it might be... Do you think something terrible has happened?... Oh, Daddy, we can't tell you how sad and desolate this makes us feel!'[13].

So it was that while Jacob mourned for his dead son, his perfectly-alive-but-not-best-pleased son was actually being displayed as prize exhibit in the Egyptian market, with cries of, 'Ooooh! Look at his teeth!'. In the market that day, Pharaoh's chief guard was looking for a young slave to do a little light dusting and feed the (sacred) cats. Joe was just the thing – and he could prattle on about his dreams as much as he liked, because Potiphar (his new boss... well, owner really) couldn't understand a word he was saying.

SLAVES R US!

---

[13] Because it didn't.

Potiphar was a fair man (well, to be honest, he had sort of olivey coloured skin and his hair was a light shade of black, but you know what I mean). He watched Joe working, and he knew a good lad when he saw one. Joe never slacked, never asked for time off and was never late on duty. Mind you, where was he going to go? He was in a foreign country, he didn't speak the language, he had no money, and he wouldn't have got time off even if he *had* asked for it. So he just threw himself into his work. Potiphar was impressed and gave Joe more and more responsibilities. It was a strange thing, Potiphar noticed, but the more involved Joe was in the running of the house, the better things went for Potiphar. It seemed an excellent arrangement all round – Potiphar got well looked after, the money from his crops was rolling in while Joe got... well, not a lot, really. But he *was* still alive, so let's be grateful for small mercies.

Potiphar wasn't the only one keeping an eye on Joe. *Mrs* Potiphar liked the finer things in life, and to her mind the new young slave was a *very* fine thing indeed. It was well known around the palace that you didn't trust Mrs P with your husband – but her own husband seemed completely oblivious to her carryings on.

Mrs P had been used to getting what she wanted, and she wanted young Joe. Imagine her surprise, then, when Joe responded to her advances with what, even in a foreign language, was clearly 'NO!'. Unfortunately, 'No' was not a word that Mrs P was used to hearing, and she continued to pester Joe day after day until he was forced to take evasive action.

This was a bit difficult. He worked in the house. Mrs P lived in the house. He just had to make sure that wherever she was, he wasn't (and vice versa). So while Mrs P was finishing off her honey and locust waffles in the kitchen, Joe would be upstairs polishing the

gold on the fixtures and fittings. If Mrs P was doing her hair in the bedroom, Joe would be out the back door checking in a delivery from a pyramid salesman.

For a while his plan worked, but then one day... Joe was alone in the house. Well, he *thought* he was alone. Potiphar was out and he was sure that Mrs P had gone to call on the Pharaohs'. He was just checking that the bedrooms had all been aired and cleaned when he felt two hands circle his waist and a soft, silky, breathy voice whispered in his ear, 'Guess who?'

Well, on the basis that Mr P's voice had broken a long time ago and, as far as anyone could tell, he didn't wear Eau de Nile perfume, Joe had a pretty good idea of the answer to that question.

The voice started to suggest to Joe all kinds of wicked things that certainly have no place in a book like this, but be assured, if you ever find yourself in the same situation, 'No!' is *always* the right answer.

Joe turned to run away, but Mrs P (of course it was her – who did you think it was, Pharaoh having a funny turn?) had a tight hold of him. He used all the arguments he had used before: Potiphar had been good to him, God wouldn't like it, he had to go and arrange the food in the pantry into alphabetical order. But none of it seemed to make any difference. 'Make me feel like a real woman,' said Mrs P. Joe grabbed a nearby toga, threw it at her and said, 'Here, iron this!' But she was not to be put off by cheap sexist remarks. Joe knew there was only one thing to do – he turned quickly and ran from the room. The bad news was that Mrs P had such a tight hold of his coat that it didn't leave the room with him. He fled to the safety of the servant's quarters, locked his door and put his bed against it – he wasn't taking any more chances.

Mrs P sat in her bedroom. She was furious. How dare some young slave make her look a fool? She had never been so insulted in all her life and she would make him pay for this if it was the last thing she did. Her eyes looked down at the coat she was holding in her hands. It was time her husband got to hear about what had been going on. Not the truth, obviously, but her version of it...

When Potiphar came home that evening, he found his wife stretched across the bed crying her eyes out (then picking them up and putting them back in again). He rushed to her side, and, between her sobs, listened to her tell the tale of good, honest Joe who had turned out to be no good and treacherous. Potiphar couldn't believe it. Surely Joe didn't think that having the run of the house meant his wife came as part of the deal. But as Mrs P continued to tell her story of how Joe had attacked her and tried to force her to...[14] he slowly accepted it.

Stunned and dazed, Potiphar sent for Joe and had him thrown into jail. Meanwhile, Mrs P dried her eyes, cleaned up her mascara and put the onion away. That had gone quite nicely. Now where was that young lad who popped in to do the gardens? It was time for some cultivating.

---

[14] Ed – Censored.

11 FAT COWS AND THIN WHEAT

GENESIS 40:1-23

Joe had been in worse situations than this. He couldn't quite remember when, but he was sure he must have been. After all, the jailer seemed quite friendly. So Joe set to work. He cleaned out the cells, put fresh straw down and helped serve the prison food. In fact, he was soon running things in prison in much the same way as he had run Potiphar's household. The jailer was quite happy to let him – having first assured Joe that there was no Mrs Jailer to mess things up.

That sorted out the days, but the nights were the worst. Joe would lie awake thinking of his dad and his brothers back home. They hadn't always got on. To be honest, as far as his brothers were concerned, they'd *never* got on, but at least they were family, and blood was thicker than water (although not the water they served in prison which had a texture and life all of its own). Joe was sure that the business with his brothers and the well had just been a misunderstanding, and as for selling him into slavery – well, it could happen to anyone. And he had been so sure about what those dreams meant...

This last thought must have been louder than he knew, for suddenly, at the far end of the cell, there was a movement in the straw. 'Rats,' thought Joe and looked for something to throw. His drinking mug was nearest, and it was only when the rat said, 'Ow, that hurt,' that Joe thought he might have made a mistake. He peered into the darkness and there coming towards him were Pharaoh's chief cook and Pharaoh's bottle-washer.

They had been in prison for so long that most people had forgotten who'd put them there in the first place. All they could remember was a big party up at the palace, lots to drink and Pharaoh getting very, very angry.

'Did you say something about dreams?' asked Cookie.

'About understanding what they meant?' added Bottle-Washer (BW to his mates). Joe wasn't sure what was coming next, but he admitted to having 'dabbled' a bit.

It turned out that these two ex-palace bods had both had strange dreams the night before, and they wondered if Joe could explain them. Joe was honest. He told them that he couldn't do it, but he was sure it wouldn't be a problem for God.

BW retold his dream. 'I was back in the palace gardens, watching the vines grow. As soon as the grapes were ready, I took a bunch, squeezed them into Pharaoh's cup and offered this Egyptian version of Beaujolais Nouveau to him.'

Joe didn't have to think for long about this. It was obvious. 'You're going to get your old job back,' he told BW. 'Pharaoh will let bygones be bygones, and you'll be bottle-washing and cup-bearing like nobody's business before the week is out.'

Cookie was agog. This was the kind of thing he had hoped for, so, in a rush, he told his dream. 'Baskets – Bread – Birds – Binge – Buzzed Off.'

'Well, I'm blowed,' thought Joe. 'How am I going to explain this one?' Cookie was looking at him hopefully. It wasn't that Joe didn't know what to say, it was more how to say it. 'Look, Cookie. It's like this,' began Joe. 'There's good news and there's bad news. The good news is you are going to get out of prison and you'll be free. Errr, the bad news is it won't be for very long. How can I put this? You'll be brown bread... errr, dead.'

BW tried not to look too relieved. Cookie tried to convince himself that Joe had probably got it wrong. But Joe hadn't, and sure enough three days later BW was back decanting the wine and passing round the hors d'oeuvres while Cookie had gone to that great bakery in the sky. You don't want to know

too much about how he died. Let's just say it involved a long sharp pole with the pointed end coming out of his mouth. As for where it went in... well, use your imagination!

As BW said his goodbyes, Joe reminded him that they'd made a deal. If Joe had got the dream right, then BW would tell Pharaoh about his friend who had been wrongfully imprisoned. 'Sure,' said BW, 'it's the first thing I'll do. How could I forget what you did for me, pal?' But he could. And he did.

Two more years went by. A lot of rats got hit by Joe's drinking mug, and a lot of prisoners had come and gone (one way or another), but Joe was still there. He was allowed out now and again to have a walk round (as long as he was back before sundown), he played a

GENESIS
41:1–43

little cards with the jailer and sometimes got two pieces of carrot in his stew. But all that was about to change.

Pharaoh had been having restless nights. He would go to sleep, but then these awful dreams wouldn't leave him alone. There were thin cows eating fat cows and small pieces of wheat gobbling up big pieces of wheat – but the thin things stayed thin! It was a dieter's dream, but it was Pharaoh's nightmare and he didn't like it one little bit.

He told his court magicians about the dreams. They consulted charts and star movements, and they did things with the entrails of chickens that were really quite disgusting, but they all came up with the same answer: 'We have no idea what these dreams mean, your Greatness!'

BW heard all this going on, and suddenly the penny dropped. He knew someone who could sort it out! What was his name? Jim, Jack, Jennifer – no that's being silly. It came to him. 'Joe!' he yelled out. Pharaoh turned and looked at him. 'You can choose from, "Your Majesty", "Your Wonderfulness" or "Your Greatness". Call me "Joe" again, and you'll be saying hello to a very sharp stick,' he said not looking too pleased. However, once BW made it clear what he was burbling on about, Pharaoh cheered up. Joe was sent for, and after a quick wash and brush up (well, not that quick – he'd been in prison a long time and it was quite some beard he had to get rid of) he presented himself before Pharaoh.

As Pharaoh sat before him, Joe was praying like he'd never prayed before. He knew God could help him out. He was certain that he would. He was sure that there wasn't any possibility of God letting him down. Was there? Like his father before him, he fell back on that powerful, universal prayer when all others fail, 'HELP!!' And help God did. Joe listened to Pharaoh recount his tale of thin cows eating fat cows

101

and still being thin cows, big wheat being snaffled up by little wheat without any change evident. As he listened, Joe was filled with excitement. He could do this one. In centuries to come, only those who had completed the last level of *Toy Story 2*, the computer game, defeated all the baddies and found all the secret rooms in record time could have known just how he felt at that particular moment.

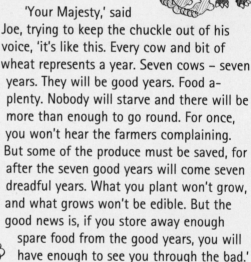

'Your Majesty,' said Joe, trying to keep the chuckle out of his voice, 'it's like this. Every cow and bit of wheat represents a year. Seven cows – seven years. They will be good years. Food a-plenty. Nobody will starve and there will be more than enough to go round. For once, you won't hear the farmers complaining. But some of the produce must be saved, for after the seven good years will come seven dreadful years. What you plant won't grow, and what grows won't be edible. But the good news is, if you store away enough spare food from the good years, you will have enough to see you through the bad.'

Pharaoh was astounded. There was something about this young man's words that had the ring of truth about them. Pharaoh asked Joe if he would like a job. Joe was thrilled and started telling Pharaoh how good he was at housework, and that he'd be happy to wash the plates in the palace kitchens if there was a vacancy. Unfortunately, Joe's grasp of Egyptian, even after all this time, was still a bit dodgy and so what Pharaoh heard was, 'I'm very good at mousework and I'd be happy to smash your plates.' Pharaoh was in too good a mood to let this worry him, though. 'I was thinking of making you Prime Minister,' he said to Joe's astonishment. 'Errr, well, I mean, that's very nice,' stammered Joe. 'But don't you have to have an election, seek the will of the people, allow the democratic process to unfold?'

Pharaoh smiled, 'Oh yes, we have a system of One Man, One Vote here. I am the one man and my one vote chooses *you* for Prime Minister.'

Even while the prison guard was chopping off his chains, and the royal wardrobe mistress was measuring him up for regal gowns, Joe couldn't quite believe what was happening. He was thirty and here he was – an outsider, a nobody with a prison record – being given the top job under Pharaoh.

12 WALK LIKE AN EGYPTIAN

GENESIS 41:44 – 42:38

It all seemed to be turning out right for Joe: freedom, a top job, a wife and even a new Egyptian name – Zaphenath Paneah (which is useful in Scrabble but not much else, so we'll continue to call him 'Joe'). Just as he said, there were seven years of bumper harvests. Joe made sure that all the spare food was stored ready for the bad years to come. There was so much to store that they even stopped recording it and just concentrated on building bigger and better warehouses.

And he was proved to not only be right about the seven good years, but also about the years that followed producing no harvest at all. Thanks to Joe's good management skills, no one in Egypt suffered. Joe was the man of the moment. As he travelled around the country, making sure that the food was being distributed fairly, he was cheered and treated like a hero. Some people even threw themselves at his feet. As Joe watched them, he couldn't help remembering the dreams he'd had as a teenager when stars and sheaves of corn bowed down. It was all coming true. Although originally, he'd thought it would be his brothers who would do the bowing down. Speaking of which...

It wasn't just Egypt that was suffering from the effects of famine. From all over the world, people were travelling to Egypt to try and buy food.

Because of Joe's insight and good sense, there was plenty to spare, so not only were the Egyptians well fed, but they were making a tidy profit on top from trading with the other countries. Canaan hadn't escaped the famine, and when Jacob heard that there was grain in Egypt, he rounded up

his sons and sent them off as quickly as possible. All of the brothers, that is, except Benjamin. If you can think that far back, you will recall that he was Rachel's other son. Jacob thought he'd lost one of her sons, and he wasn't willing to risk the only one left.

WHY DON'T WE JUST ORDER IN SOME PIZZA?

The brothers arrived in Egypt and were sent, as foreigners, to make their request to the man in charge of food distribution, who, of course, was none other

than Joe. They didn't recognise him, though. It never occurred to them to make a connection between the smart, sophisticated man in front of them and the pain-in-the-neck teenager that they'd sold all those years ago. Joe, on the other hand, recognised them straight away. It's funny how being thrown into a well and sold into slavery leaves an impression on your memory. Joe made sure that he only spoke to his brothers through his interpreter. It might have looked a bit odd if they'd realised he could speak their language. It also meant that he could understand every word they said to each other, without them knowing.

Joe had come a long way since that day he'd spent down the well. He'd learned to trust God, and seen things work out for him in ways that he would never have dared imagine. Nonetheless, there was still a bit of him that wanted to make his brothers suffer for what they'd done. Not very nice – but would you have acted any differently?

ERM?... YOU'RE MINCE PIES!??

'You're spies,' he accused them (via his interpreter). 'You just want to look round in order to make plans for attacking us.' The brothers were astonished. Maybe something was getting lost in the translation, so they tried again. They told Joe about their family – their father and younger brother at home and their other brother who was dead. 'Prove it,' said Joe, and ordered them to be locked up for three days while they considered his demands. Now three days in prison, and the thought that you really do need to get hold of some food does wonders for sharpening the mind. Sure enough, after three days they were quite willing to go and fetch Ben, and until they returned they would leave Simeon in prison. They were determined to return... at least Simeon hoped that they were.

106

If truth be told, the brothers were scared. They had expected to make a quick trip to Egypt, buy some food, and go home. But here they were being accused of all kinds of things. They couldn't help wondering if God was punishing them for what they had done to Joe all those years ago. Which was what was happening – only by Joe, not by God.

They were given grain to take back with them, and set off to find Jacob and Ben. Surely, they thought, as they travelled along, things couldn't get any worse? But they could. The brothers stared open-mouthed when they opened their sacks of grain for there, lying on top of each sack, was the money they had used to pay for the food. It was all very strange – strange that is, unless you'd seen Joe telling his servants to put the money in the sacks before they left.

EGYPT IS INCREDIBLE...

When they got home, the brothers rushed in to tell their dad, Jacob, their news, each speaking over the other to chip in their bit of the story.

 GOVERNOR WAS A BIT RUDE THOUGH...

 FOOD EVERYWHERE...

 BUT HE DID GIVE US PLENTY OF GRAIN...

 AND WE STILL SEEM TO HAVE THE MONEY...

 CAN'T REALLY EXPLAIN THAT...

 BUT THERE'S SOMETHING ELSE...

 IT WASN'T OUR FAULT...

 HE WOULDN'T LET US COME BACK OTHERW...

This was Jacob, who for an old man still had plenty of breath in his lungs. 'Where's Simeon?' he asked.

The brothers told the tale – how Simeon was in prison and would only be released if Benjamin was taken to Egypt.

Jacob wasn't having this. There had been too many sons going missing round here, and he wasn't going to risk another. The brothers pleaded with their father. They already felt that God was having a go at them, and if they could only put things right a little bit, they would feel a whole lot better.

Jacob was adamant: 'Never, not at all, in no circumstances, absolutely not, over my dead body, nix, nein, non, NO WAY!'

'We'll take that as a "No" then,' said Reuben.

13 A DREAM COME TRUE

GENESIS 43:1–34

The famine continued, the grain was eaten and Jacob went on saying, 'No,' until eventually even he had to accept that they needed more food, and that they weren't going to get any unless Benjamin went along to Egypt as well. Finally, Jacob agreed, but this time there must be no possibility of being mistaken for spies. They were to take gifts of honey, pistachio nuts and almonds. Furthermore the money had to be returned for the first lot of grain – with interest. Jacob was not willing to take any chances.

SO I NEED TO CUT IT INTO THIRTEEN SLICES?!!

WOW! THAT'S LOVELY HONEY!

WHY THANK YOU, DARLING!

Asking whether the brothers were nervous about what would happen when they got to Egypt is like asking whether a duck with one leg swims round in circles, or whether the Pope's a Catholic, or... well, anyway, believe me they were. Imagine their surprise, then, when the governor invited them to his house and prepared a meal for them. When they offered him the money for the first lot of grain

he said he'd already had it. 'Maybe that God of yours is looking after you,' he said. The brothers were no longer nervous – just confused. However, they were glad to see Simeon again (but not as glad as *he* was to see *them*).

They produced their gifts for Joe and bowed down to the ground. Joe didn't know if he wanted to laugh or cry – it was his dream come true. But there would be a time for laughing and that time had

not yet come. When Joe saw Benjamin, it was not laughter but tears that he had to control. The last time he had seen his little brother, Ben was just a boy, and now here he was a man. Joe rushed off to his room until the tears had dried up, and then returned and ordered the banquet to begin.

The brothers were stunned. Last time it was all suspicion and accusations. Now it was smiles, good food and friendly service. Strange but true. However, just as everything looked as though it was going to turn out right for them, it was about to go horribly wrong...

The sacks of grain were being prepared for the brothers to take back to Canaan. Once again, Joe made sure that their money was put in the sacks and this time he added a little extra gift of his own – his special silver drinking cup. He had one more plan, to check out whether or not his brothers had really changed since that memorable day all those years ago.

GENESIS 44:1-34

The brothers left, but Joe sent some of his servants after them. When the brothers were stopped on their way home by Joe's men, they were still so overwhelmed by his change in attitude that they assumed he'd sent some more gifts for them. However, the cries of 'Stop thieves!' somehow didn't have that friendly ring about them.

When they were accused of stealing the silver cup, the brothers protested their innocence. 'Search our sacks, but if anyone has the cup, you can kill him here and now,' they protested. Bad move, cos guess whose sack the cup was in? That's right – young Ben's! As the

brothers returned to Egypt, a more dispirited group of people it would have been difficult to find (although you could try standing outside the ground after an England football international and watching the home crowd). There was just one thought going through the brothers' minds – to lose one of your father's favourite sons is a misfortune, but to lose *both* begins to look like downright stupidity. Even being told that Ben wouldn't be killed, but would simply become a palace slave didn't cheer anyone up. 'Might as well be dead as far as Dad's concerned,' thought Reuben.

'Yeah,' thought Judah, '*we* might as well all be dead.'

'Hey,' thought Reuben, 'stop crowding my thoughts.'

The brothers bowed in front of Joseph. Judah made the case for their innocence:

- They'd been framed;
- It wasn't them;

– They weren't there;
– It must have been eleven other brothers!

When this didn't work, Judah offered himself instead of Ben. 'Keep *me* as a slave. Ben wouldn't have done this thing. Besides, if he doesn't go back home our father won't survive the shock.'

Joe thought of a time when, over twenty years before, these brothers would have done anything to make a bit of money and, if people (like him) got in their way, they 'arranged' something. Now here they were, prepared to do anything to keep their father from further grief. Joe may have travelled the furthest in terms of geography and status, but it looked as though his brothers had been on quite a journey also. They'd had plenty of shocks for one day, but now it was time for one more.

Joe looked at his brothers who, heads down low, were waiting for the reply to Judah's offer. There was a long silence. The servants had left the room, and with each passing moment, the brothers feared the worst.

GENESIS
45:1-28

What they didn't expect was for this Egyptian leader to burst into tears! What the protocol was for such situations, they didn't know. Should they politely ignore it? Offer him a handkerchief? Look the other way? Or join in out of sympathy? While they were still thinking about this, they had a further shock. He was talking to them. Well, he'd done that before – but never in their own language. And what he was saying made everything else that had happened that day seem like just everyday,

run-of-the-mill stuff.

The brothers looked at each other. They must have misheard, but the look on everyone's face told them that they'd all heard the same thing.

It took a while, but finally Joe told them all that had happened since the day the brothers had traded with the Ishmaelites: working for Potiphar, the false accusations, time in jail, interpreting Pharaoh's dreams, taking the top job in Egypt and now this. It all seemed a bit of a dream itself, but the brothers were convinced – stunned, astounded, amazed, boggled and flabbergasted, but convinced.

Together they marvelled at a God who could take evil actions and bring good out of every one of them.

Now Joe wanted to bring the whole family together again. There was plenty of room and food in Egypt, and he gave orders for the brothers to return and bring the wives, children, servants and especially Jacob back to stay.

GENESIS
46:1 – 47:26

Back in Canaan, Jacob counted the brothers twice to make sure that they had all returned. That came to twenty-two so that was wrong.

Next, he tried counting the legs and dividing by two: he got eleven, so that was all right then. Mind you, counting was difficult. They wouldn't keep still, and kept jabbering on about Joseph. It was a bit cruel to taunt an old man with thoughts of his long-lost son. Slowly, however, as the brothers calmed down, the message began to get through. Joe was alive – not only alive, but

holding the top job in Egypt, with wealth beyond imagining –
alive and kicking, in fact.

It took a while
to pack everything
up, but as soon as
they could, the
whole family were
moving on to new
ground. On the way,
Jacob stopped and
talked to God –
there was one thing
bothering him. It

JUST IN CASE WE
GET HUNGRY ON THE WAY!

would be marvellous to see Joe again, and the land they were
going to sounded terrific. But Jacob had been so sure that
Canaan was the place God had marked out for them, just as Isaac
and Abraham had been before him. It seemed wrong, somehow,
to be turning their backs on what God had promised, just for a
place in the sun and three square meals a day.

God spoke clearly to Jacob. He had
given the land of Canaan to Jacob's family
and the time would come when they would
return. God's purposes might seem to take a
while to work themselves out, but worked
out they will be. When the time was right,
Jacob's family would return. Before then,
there was the new land to enjoy and a
family reunion to take place.

Reassured, Jacob moved on and when
they came to Goshen – the land Pharaoh had
given to Joe's family – there was a man
who despite the royal regalia, the foreign
haircut and the strange accent, still had his
mother's eyes and smile. Jacob had no
doubts at all. This was Joseph. He reached

117

out his arms to embrace him, and we shall draw the curtains and let them meet in private.

14 LAST BITES

Well, that's about it. The family were all reunited and enjoyed seventeen more years with Jacob before he followed family tradition and died. Before that though, he prayed for Joe's two sons: Manasseh and Ephraim. History repeated itself as he blessed first the younger son (Ephraim) and then the older (Manasseh). Joe wanted his dad to do it the other way round, but Jacob was sure that this was what God wanted. Jacob knew by now that God could always work things out, even when tradition and convention weren't followed.

Joe was richer than anyone else in Egypt (apart from Pharaoh) and had forgiven his brothers all that had happened in the past. True, they thought he might change once Jacob was no longer around, but they needn't have worried. Despite the awful things that had happened to him, Joe could see that God had never left him and his sufferings were part of a bigger plan. He didn't know where it would all end, but if God was looking after things, he reckoned it would be a good place.

By the time Joe died, his children had children. Then those children had children, and to be quite honest, it was a bit tricky to remember all the names[15]. One thing was clear though. From those days decades before, when Abraham had worried about having no children at all, there had been quite a change. They were quite a family.

There was Abraham, wandering off to strange lands, and trying to sacrifice his only son. Then Jacob, cheating and twisting his way to success. And as for Joe, who would have thought that the slave boy in prison would become a leading figure in a great nation? It's a funny thing, but when God makes promises, somehow the promises come true. Not the way you would expect, and sometimes it takes longer than you hoped, but so far, although many people in Joe's family had made mistakes, God hadn't slipped up once.

---

[15] Thank goodness Christmas hadn't been invented!

God loved Abraham, Joe and even Jake. He loved them enough to take them on journeys of discovery and danger, where they experienced uncertainties and the unexpected. Not for his own amusement. Not just to make them better people (though it did). But to create a family, no, bigger than that, a nation who would show the rest of the world how to serve the true God – in their worship, and in the whole of their lives.

So it was that Joseph died knowing that God was in control. With his final breath, he asked that his body wouldn't be left forever in Egypt. If God had meant them to live in Canaan, then they would live in Canaan when the time was right and he didn't want to be left behind.

Who could have guessed that before the family of Abraham, Isaac, Jacob and Joseph was to see God's promised land there would be dreadful suffering for them all? There would be times of murder, plague, pestilence and sadness, but that is another tale for another day[15]. For now, we must creep away from the Egyptian palace where a family is gathered round the body of Joseph, someone who dreamed big dreams and lived to see those dreams come true. And as we go, let's not forget that God dreams even bigger dreams – for Joseph's family, for you and me, for the whole world. Dreams of nations working with other nations. Dreams where war is a thing of the past. Dreams where men, women, boys and girls will follow not their own thoughts and desires but allow God's dreams to be lived out in their everyday lives.

I wonder what would happen if everyone said tomorrow morning, 'Please God, show me your dreams for my life'? I wonder what would happen if you did? Go on, I dare you.

---

[15] Read what happened next in *A Red Sea, a Burning Bush and a Plague of Frogs.*

WHO ARE THESE GUYS?

MALC'

Schools-worker, charity coordinator, youth pastor, local radio celebrity, church minister are just some of the 'work experience' that Malc' can fill in on a CV. He has also, at different times, had an ear pierced and dyed his hair green. He devours books, films and black coffee in between working for a church in Coventry, studying in Oxford and socialising with anyone who will talk to him. He has written for SU's *Quest* Bible notes and *SALT* material and now, of course, the blockbuster *Bible Bites* series.

IAN

Shropshire lad, Ian, was born and brought up on a small sheep farm. His childhood dislike of the outdoors, lack of computer games, the everlasting rain and his phobia of chickens (linked to a vicious attack by 300 manic hens when he was four) led him to the drawing board and he's been drawing ever since. Despite his early acquaintances being mainly of the four-legged variety, Ian has progressed through a variety of academic institutions and is now a trainee solicitor working in Sheffield, where he worships at St Thomas's Church.

A Red Sea, a Burning Bush and a Plague of Frogs

In the second book published in the *Bible Bites* series, meet Moses who walked through the sea without getting his feet wet, and who made Pharaoh into a frog-millionaire. I liked it so much I bought fifty copies... but then I ate them all. Belch.

Available from your local Christian bookshop. Or direct from:
S U (Mail Order), PO Box 5148, Milton Keynes MLO, MK2 2YX
Tel: 01908 856006 Fax: 01908 856 020 www.scriptureunion.org.uk

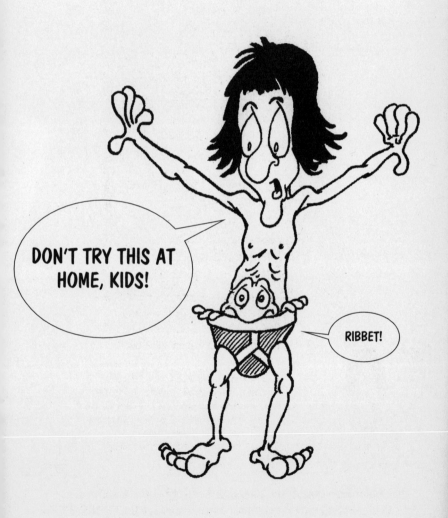

A Giant, a Crown and an Open-air Bath

FROM SOME OF OUR READERS:

Bible bites books are really different and a fun thing to read.

Some of the pictures remind me of my mum!

I never knew they had kebabs in the Bible.

I love the Bible Bites books. They're brilliant! Please do lots more.

It's great to have books like these to help you understand what the Bible is saying.